Fallen Sky, Bought and Sold

A Poetry Collection

By David Greshel

© 2018 David Greshel
A Neon Sunrise Publication. All Rights Reserved

Introduction

There's a process to writing. That seems obvious right? We don't just magically produce a complete piece out of thin air like a practiced illusionist (at least I don't, do you? Am I the only one without magic writing mojo?) All these words, ideas, and thoughts spin around in your head and your imagination seizes upon certain ones and connects them to others to form statements and considers the structure or appearance and then you sit down somewhere and pour it all out onto a piece of paper or a digital screen…a process. It looks different depending on who's in the chair, but we all have a process we work through when the serendipity of inspiration flashes before us. But what happens when the imagination is dormant, when inspiration is absent? When the well just seems to be sun scorched and empty? That also looks a bit different for every writer, but for me I found that writing prompts helped to kick start the creative process. Having a kind of timeframe with the monthly prompts also helped to keep the juices flowing and the results are now collected here.

All of the pieces on the following pages are the result of writing prompt challenges that I participated in on Instagram between September of 2015 and March of 2017. In a given month, there are probably dozens of different challenges being offered in a multitude of styles so there is something out there for everyone. The writing community is always growing and I've made some great connections over the years with some amazingly talented people. Social media as a whole is a bit of a mixed bag and can easily send you careening off into incredibly dark places, but the Instagram challenges provided a creative outlet that fed an artistic desire for feedback and a human need for connection.

Inspiration is tricky business sometimes, and every writer I know has experienced writer's block in some form. The prompt challenges provided unique opportunities to explore different ideas and even turn a few established ones upside down. The process of forming a complete thought and idea that turned into a full piece brought life out of what might have otherwise been a dry season for me. It was liberating, in a way, to have this list of ideas to ponder and turn over in my head to come up with something in my own voice knowing that a lot of people would also be approaching the same prompts. Most of the time, I wanted to approach the given prompt in a way that was outside the norm…and I would say I succeeded in that approach, but I'll leave that up to my readers.

I had an absolute blast working through the prompts included here, and I'm happy to have this collection complete and in your hands. I hope it finds you well and that you enjoy the time you spend with these words. I would also encourage you to try your hand at a few of the prompts yourself and see what you're inspired to create, and I would love to see what you come up with if you're willing to share!

See you where the sidewalk ends,

David
July 13th, 2018

Acknowledgements

As much as I support and strive for a DIY ethos in creating and publishing, producing a book is not a solo effort. Sure, I do the heavy lifting of crafting the words and phrases into something that resembles poetry, but that's only part of the story. There's also editing, cover design, marketing and promotions, and a host of other things that I cannot do alone – well not and keep my sanity intact. With that in mind, I would like to show my great appreciation for the following:

God, through whom all innate creative desire is ultimately derived. Thank you for the talents and life that you have blessed me with and thank you for the ultimate gift of your Son.

My Family and friends – you keep me going and provide the connection we so desperately need as human beings. I love you all and thank you for always providing the encouragement and positive criticism needed to stretch and grow.

Travis Gibb – Thank you for sharing your marketing and web design expertise, for all of your support and encouragement as I develop Neon Sunrise into a full-fledged publishing company, and for your friendship.

My City of Refuge and Rev Reality extended family – Thank you for loving me well and for being a community I'm proud to be a part of. Let's change the world by sharing that love.

My cat Pantera – just for being awesome.

The Instagram writing community – Thank you for the support and encouragement; and thank you for the inspiration when the well has seemed dry. Things have definitely changed since I joined the platform in 2012, but it definitely still holds the potential for positive influence. Keep writing and sharing, you all have unique voices that the world needs to hear.

I also want to provide special recognition for the following people who created the writing prompts for the challenges I participated in:

When We Outgrow Our Bones - September 2015
As Everything Turns Grey - November 2016

J.R. Rogue - @j.r.rogue
Kat Savage - @kat.savage

DNS Poetry Challenges – August and September 2016

Angeline Roberts - @through.the.ghost
Ruby Stein - @swallow_down_satan

December Falls Poetry Challenge – December 2016

Ashley Jane - @breath_words_
Matt Shirley - @aseawords

Mad March Poetry Challenge – March 2017

Raven of the Writing Desk - @ravenofthewritingdesk

Each of these individuals is a talented writer in their own right, and you should definitely check out their work and follow them on Instagram.

Thank you all again for the inspiration and for sharing your unique writing gifts with the world!

I was unable to determine who hosted the challenges I participated in for February and March of 2016, but my thanks goes out to them also

When We Outgrow Our Bones
September 2015

1. Swimming like a Cinder Block
2. Artery Art
3. Hope in a Helium Tank
4. Gambits
5. In the Break Room
6. My Red Converse & You
7. Lipstick & Illusions
8. Tabula Rasa
9. House of Cards
10. Feather Cages
11. Lonely Layers of Lace
12. Collarbone Symphonies
13. Plastic Feelings
14. Weltschmerz
15. Lackluster Mistakes
16. Sticky Sorrows
17. Lungs like Deflated Balloons
18. The Devil, Denial, & Day Terrors
19. Paper Thin Promises
20. Skin Prison Sins
21. Be the Villain
22. Sternum Scars & Secrets
23. Cardboard Gravestones
24. In Case You Forgot
25. Singing the Broken Glass Blues
26. Our Ink
27. One Way Ticket
28. Resplendent
29. I Met You There
30. On Rogues & Savages

Prompt: Swimming like a Cinder Block

The World is One, and all That

September sauntered in
Stealthily signaling summer's
Vain glorious inevitable end
Amidst humid sun strokes
And languid divination

Such rabid disbelief abounds
Conjuring drowning bubbles
Swimming cinderblocks
And glacial sonic booms

Daydream national anthem
Wake me when the curtain drops
Exit, stage left

Prompt: Artery Art

Side Salad Surgery

Carve myself open
With all the practiced finesse
Of a back-alley butcher
Stalking the shadowed unwary
Chest cracked and gaping wide
Ripped, scarred, exposed
Heart strung out
Gushing arterial art
With every sanguine thought
Painting crimson strokes
In the absent afterthought
Of your foregone conclusions
And misplaced intentions
Parading through all these
Exhausted lines
That we never once believed

Prompt: Hope in a Helium Tank

You Can't Release Only One

A vibrant azure palette
Enveloping life's horizon
Golden rays illuminating
Every waking thought
Every passing dream
Gazing into painted orbs
Awash in sleek bends
Latex curves
All the promise of hope
Bound up
In a fleeting helium tank
So close to expiration
And divinity interrupted
Melting in the pause
Of our rainbow escape pod

Chess in Six Dimensions

Alight in the embers
Smoldering in the atmosphere
Weightless in the moment
Tireless...delirious
Calculating infinity
And beyond

Rendering nonsensical phrases
Into punctuated gambits
Orchestrated by pyromaniacs
Let loose in volcanic abandon

Transfiguration in the instant
Sentient ex nihilo
Cogito ergo sum
The mystery begins anew

Prompt: In the Break Room

Any Given Tuesday Afternoon

Faded marketing ploys
Decorate porous cork board
Yellow curling pages scream
Enticing diet fads
"Gently used" bikes for sale
The office Christmas party
You will never forget
Though the taste refused to linger
The moment eclipsed
Drowned in missed calls
Budget meetings at three
Carefully avoided glances
And a facade of indifference
Yet it drives blades
Heart rending agony
Every time she speaks

Prompt: My Red Converse & You

Dancing Angels in Costello Melodies

The fuzzed out speakers
Hummed and crackled
In the evening autumn breeze
Dialed into classics
Remembering we were young
With Costello crooning about
Angels wearing my shoes
Laugh about it even now
Watching you dancing
In my crimson Chuck T's
Goofy smile and a cotton shirt
The only other things between us

What I wouldn't give
To be there watching you again

Prompt: Lipstick & Illusions

You Never Forget Your First Mirage

My first love (lust?)
A murder poet in delirium
Swaying lines drawing eyes
Mesmerized in perfect curves
Beckoning in samba time
Every waking sense alive
In smoldering stolen glances
And liquid lipstick bruises

Daydream illusions
Dissipating in distraction
And the weight of desire
Never truly realized

Tabula Rasa Starter Kits

Early Sunday mornings
Lurching back to life
In the slinky torrid wake
Of another Saturday night
Spent repurposing my liver
And drowning every memory
I ever saved of you

Desert gravel mouth
Thunder crushed temples
Behind bloodshot eyes
Primary waking sensations
No one has requested

Never. Drinking. Again.

Prompt: House of Cards

Million Dollar House of Cards

Balanced so precariously
This monumental deceit
Stretched between indifference
And arrogance
One might wonder what force
It takes to maintain
Such a mammoth structure
What sort of binding agent
Seals clever limbs to joints
Turns hearts
Buys support

My tongue on overdrive
Spinning these silken webs
Singing this siren song
Yet it would all come crashing down
With a single truthful word

Prompt: Feather Cages

Second Guessing Sunshine

I felt the rising breeze
Streaming down from the north
To streak through iron hills
Bearing the essence of spring

Standing on the edge
Of a seaside cliff
Limbs stretched and caged
In wax and feathers

Leaning in
Leaping towards the horizon
Diving for my freedom
I am Icarus in flight

Prompt: Lonely Layers of Lace

Residential Spelunking

Weekend attic treasure hunt
Signaling the demise of summer
Stifled in the musty gloom
Single naked bulb
Illuminating cardboard towers
And forgotten bicycle racks

Cracking the lonely layers
Of dust and scotch tape
Revealing love letter memories
Bound in silk and lace
Rekindling dormant flames
Recalling you from space

Prompt: Collarbone Symphonies

Sunday Morning Observations

Sunlight streaking through
Piercing the window blinds
Throwing illumination
Across this drowsy bedroom
Eyes alive and adjusting
Glancing to the side
Recalling a favorite song
Naked beside you
Kissing clavicle curves
Fingertips trailing
Tracing empty pillowcases
The bed is far too big
Every night that you're gone

Prompt: Plastic Feelings

Lemmings Leading the Blind

Practiced facades held firm
Masking any semblance
Of truth in this reality
Placating all these inquiries
With perfect plastic feelings
Emotive expectations
Unconcerned with any part
That lies beneath this charade
Never think
Never question
Just smile and obey

Prompt: Weltschmerz

Can't Rain All the Time....or Something Like That

Steel gray canopy spread wide
Masking any inkling of light
In this season of leaden ennui
Punctuated by gnawing realizations
And Satisfaction on the stereo
Sick and tired of living
With people
Who are sick and tired
Of people
Who never seem to admit
That life is not their isolated experience

Prompt: Lackluster Mistakes

Misadventures in Might've Been

All the ways I could count
These ones and zeroes
Numbering past regrets
Rank and file penance stare
You'd hardly make the list
Maybe just below those times
I ignored 'what not to wear'

Prompt: Sticky Sorrows

Candyland Confessions

Molasses swamp invaded
Exploding over reality
In heralded despair
Trapping sweet surroundings
Binding lollipop laments
And banking on the luck of the draw

Dammit stuck again

Prompt: Lungs like Deflated Balloons

Drowning in the White Noise

Imaginary opposition stacked
Towering in the dying sun
Insurmountable
Unbelievable
Overwhelming tide of dread
Transfixed
Immobilized
Lungs in full collapse
Asphyxiation realized
Compulsive anxiety bleeding
Into every word you speak

Prompt: The Devil, Denial, & Day Terrors

Overactive Imagination, Don't You Ever Take a Day Off?

This never happened
Nothing in our tangled history
To prove this pointed exchange
No elusive might've been
To frame these incisive seconds
Tearing gushing holes in my chest
Center mass
Never happened
Never...

Devilish whispers
Invading
Caressing
Convincing

...But what if?

Prompt: Paper Thin Promises

<Insert Names> 2016

I am forever amazed at the ease
Of these deceitful twists
That roll so smoothly
From your practiced tongue
Painting with your ancient native language
A torrid tale of flattery
And patriotic conquest
Demonized opposition
Apocalyptic ammunition

All the empty green promises
Rice paper thin and shredded
Worthless like all the rest

Prompt: Skin Prison Sins

<u>One Hundred Million and Counting</u>

It's always in the indigo deep
Of midnight's embrace
That your memory preys upon
My dreamless insomnia
Stalking every tossing turn
With pointed reminders
Of all the faded ecstasy
Spent entwined in secret
Enraptured in illicit desire
Explosive ruptured aftermath
Imprisoned in the hangover
Morning after horizon
Feedback loop repeat

One more night
Of flesh and bone

Prompt: Be the Villain

The Much Anticipated Heel Turn

Spaceflight comet jockey
Racing meteor showers
In A-minor movements
Punctuated by deviation
And antiquated illumination

Burn it all to ash and cinders
Leave nothing to linger
No misplaced saccharine
Romantic allusions

I am the villain in this story

Prompt: Sternum Scars & Secrets

All Those Clever Girls

Silhouetted in silver sparks
Showered among salivating seas
Awash on sugar sand beaches
And standing sabal palms

Framed nocturnal explorations
Erected under
Lunar illusions
In their final exposition
The last secret
I never told

There is no heart left
Only scars

Prompt: Cardboard Gravestones

Saturday Afternoon Matinee

Visions of valleys quaking
Rumbling in aftershocks
And annihilation waves
Leaving scattered litter
Cardboard headstones
Marking nameless graves
Washed away in the downpour
Detritus in passing
Cannon fodder for the moment
Event horizon imminent

"Wake up Sarah
You're dreaming again..."

Prompt: In Case You Forgot

Red House Painters in Reverse

Playful reminders in jest
Calculated recollections
Left in obvious locations
"In case you forgot"
She said...

Many things I've misplaced
A few bits neglected
Phone numbers
To do lists
The odd deadline or two

But I've never forgotten a single thing
I ever learned about you

Prompt: Singing the Broken Glass Blues

Call Me Hercules Lead Belly

It's never enough to satisfy
Every sensation haunts me
With an aching lust for more
And I hunger...

Every task set down is past
Twelve labors and counting
Crawling across these miles
Of broken shattered glass
Singing the timeless blues
And pleading for just one more
Agonizing taste of you...

Prompt: Our Ink

Bards and Jesters, Aren't We All?

Restless autumn evenings
Permeated with punctuation
Wrestling wild sentences
Into any sort of
Comfortable submission
That holds these subtle dreams
In well-worn narratives
And eccentric traditions
Telling tall tales
Through the ink in this pen
Through the ink on our skin
Such lovely fables
Without any sort of an end

Prompt: One Way Ticket

The Lonely Realization

I guess it was always cold here
Not in temperature
But reception
That sense you just had enough
And were tired of trying
I'm tired of fighting
Last night
Last call
Woke up naked and alone
Scribbled apologies
Next to airline receipts
One way to Rome

I guess you can go home again

Prompt: Resplendent

Chimeras by Lamplight

Did I somehow dream you up?
Breathe you into existence
In the space between
Fantasy and lucidity?
Are you a vain imaginary?

Mother Nature in all her
Virgin sunrise
Resplendent finery
Does not compare
To the radiance kept
Within your breast

You are a brilliant beacon
And I
A blind man in the making

Prompt: I Met You There

Romantic Advice from the Cure

Standing on a beach
Staring at the sea
An album on full rotation
Through so many college nights
Spent pretending to study
Dreaming of lonely coeds
Looking for more than just
Passing nightly affairs
And I met you there
Nestled in the vinyl grooves
Spinning tall tales
And deadly diagrams
That fueled imagination overload

And I see you still
Every time the needle drops
Kissing wax
And filling another autumn evening

Galaxies Plus Time and Distance

Charming a way into nowhere
Silver tongue lulling
Savage hearts to submission
And eroding glacial walls
With an underlying dichotomy
Roguish wit on full display
Cocksure and humble
Embodied in this
Immortal lover's profession

"I know"

February Writing Challenge
February 2016

1. Unwilling Heart
2. Special Friend
3. Children
4. Lost Souls
5. Twin Flames
6. Love at First Sight
7. Death
8. Moon and Stars
9. Appetite
10. Roses
11. Heartbreak
12. Soul Speaks
13. Angels and Devil
14. Valentine Love
15. Coward
16. Selfish Love
17. Ignorant
18. Lose Tides
19. Ocean
20. Happiness
21. Galaxy
22. Understanding
23. Lost
24. Missing Heart
25. Courage
26. Relationship
27. Burning Flame
28. Lust
29. The Enemy

Prompt: Unwilling Heart

But When it's Done All Bets are Off

Overcome with such an elevated sense
Of empirical déjà vu
Autopilot instinct tingling in imagined extremities
Engaging hollow familiarity
And the comfort of this vanishing shade

I can feel the whispered warmth
Caressing tender aural orifices
With lilting lullabies
Drawing deeper slumber
Over drowsy eyelids
Beckoning the rest eternal

Floating in the space between
Embracing overdrive
With this stolen heart crashing
Beat after bloody beat
Unwilling to surrender
'til this work is finally done

Prompt: Special Friend

Weekends and the Art of Animal Friends

Spears of amber dawn light
Slashing through curtain folds
Shrinking slumber's shadows
Long before audio reminders
Pierce the languid Sunday silence

Blurry crusted vision
Slowly calibrated to shifting illumination
As a tiny form shifts beside me
Stretching…yawning
Pinpricks kneading through woolen blankets
Ultimate contentment rumbling
In feline appreciation

Explosion interrupting
Four paws crashing into lazy bodies
In a flurry of canine kisses
And infectious excitement
Yielding improv laughter
In the company of special friends
Breathing life into limbs
And warmth into hearts
Long thought lost to oblivion

Prompt: Children

Monday Morning and Other Horrors

Deconstructing aimless mythologies
Bent on reimagining idle pedagogies
And dragging damning indiscretions
Into the searing light of revelation
At the seat of absolute authority

The road stretches ever onward
Populated with weary travelers
And haunted refugees
The unavoidable children of war and strife
Displaced misbegotten life
Shrinking in the hands
Of omniscient reality
Imparting new creations
In the remaining detritus

Prompt: Lost Souls

Imaginary Heartbreak and Other Films

Hyacinth houses framed in idyllic landscape
Unfolding along quiet streets
Of stereotypical suburban Americana
Wrapped in nostalgic phenomenon
Catering to the languid notions
Of these unicorn lost souls
Left in time forgotten marketplaces
Trading life for eternal sobriety
In the mouth of civility
Wearing imprisonment like some trophy
Earned in the wake of imagined humility

Prompt: Twin Flames

Speaking Gemini in Solitude

Gazing out into the deepening expanse
Of multiversal galaxies
Alive with infinite possibilities
Awakening strange imaginations
And unyielding desires
Unsatisfied by the limited sensations
Sight and sound possess
Dreaming up the taste of stardust
Aching for the touch
Of Gemini flames entwined in comet tails
Streaking past the heart of solar kisses
Burning in the dead of night

Prompt: Love at First Sight

<u>Looking for New Ways to Turn a Phrase</u>

Soul enlightenment unwinding
Revealing long covered fables
Silenced in the underwhelming search
For secret analogies and hidden artistry

Savoring every subtle minutia
Caressing lines and curves discovered
No crevice left unexplored
Or shadow allowed to remain

It's somewhere there in the distance
The ever-elusive notion
Of undeniable love
In the very first moment
That vision finally appears

Prompt: Death

Seeking Wisdom, Finding None

"Nil luibh na leigheas in aghaidh an bhais"

Struck with what can only be
A sense of befuddled anxiety
As these obscure sounds bounce
Through ear canals and straining synapses
Invoking secret decoder rings
And ancient underwater honeybees
Buzzing into hollow epiphanies
Not quite fully realized
And barely imagined
In the ever-present passing moment
Sliding away in months and then years
Silently feeding insurmountable fears
And it all comes careening
To a crashing revelation
With one final breath

"There is no herb or cure for death"

Prompt: Moon and Stars

Skywriters and the Art of the Punchline

Enchanted
Transfixed in the instance
Bound to some sense of voltaic honor
Rippling through every pulse
Echoing between beats
Laced with fire erupting in bold profession
Setting flames to every ear in range
And I will tear the very moon and stars
From their heavenly places
If that's what it takes
To make you believe this proclamation
I've been screaming from the moment
Of our connection

Prompt: Appetite

Monsters and their Fear of the Dark

It's only a single moment in span
That singular instant that sparks a doubt
A tiny flicker on the widened horizon

Nearly imperceptible
Barely believable
Hardly worth ink in the ledger
Or a mention on paper

But…it…is…there
Gnawing and ravenous
Insatiable appetite
Begging for the merest taste
Of deflated ego
Or misdirected pride

And I will starve its every impulse
'til nothing but a withered husk remains
'cause it wouldn't hesitate to devour me
With half a chance to spare

Prompt: Roses

Sweet, By Any Other Name

Awakened realizations dawning over eons
Mostly spent chasing chimera apparitions
Melting in the hazy fog massed over soggy moors
Enveloping every careless dream left alone
And lost to the sweeping darkness

Caught fleeting glimpses of unfolding roses
Felt the familiar bite of their thorns
Encircling tired flesh
Lived through several lifetimes of demons
For that one fading remembrance
Of my lonely angel's first kiss

Prompt: Heartbreak

Thoughts in the Line of a King

Shattered remnants strewn over barren plains
Scattered and separated
Megaton aftermath
Annihilation serenade
Hitched a ride on the whirlwind resolution
Landed in the realm of twilight suns

Thoughts of simply laying here
Resigned to watch the world explode
It would be so easy
Not to care…not to feel
To give up the hope of anything real

Surrendering to slumber's call
Collecting stars warm from their fall
And accepting this season
As just another sojourn
On the steps of heartbreak hotel

Prompt: Soul Speaks

Communication...Ancient and Innovative

Pulsating rhythmic devices
Bleeding through strains of harmonic foundations
Entwined in melodic celebrations
Contrasting humming dissonance squirming down
Spinal columns in concert with gyrating hips
Brushing bold in hypnotic erotic suggestion
Hesitation in the briefest instant of the drop
Erupting forth with thunderous acclaim
And ecstatic aural projection
Transmitting curious astral sensations
Travelling without moving
Transfixed in the illumination
Of our interwoven souls speaking in unison
With neophyte tongues and eternal voices

Prompt: Angels and Devil

Hell is Pointless Repetition…or is it Other People?

Predisposed to repetitive vitality
Evident in these self-eroded footpaths
Through yearly timeshare territories
Predictably prophetic self-fulfillment
Sleepwalking in ¾ minor keys

I just want to incinerate it all
And leave it behind
Surrender to impulse
Reclaim some spark of savage rage
And wander out into the unknown wild
Listening for the rush of angels' wings
Or the elusive devil whispers

Anything is better
Than this Groundhog Day existence

Prompt: Valentine Love

Saints in Love, Valentine or Otherwise

There was no warning to its onset
No stoppage or emergency shut off
No tidal walls…clever dam
No carefully constructed barriers
To turn back this violent emotion
Rampaging through every icy vein
Drowning all this practiced rationale
Shouting down adopted Vulcan logic
In lieu of reckless feelings unleashed
Overwhelming every sensation uncovered

This is love
Unabashed and unconcerned
Casting off any comfort
In habitual solitude
Seeking the primal wild light
That flickers out in the shrinking distance
A beacon…a siren
A moonlight sonata
Recalling my immortal beloved
My forever Valentine

Prompt: Coward

Billy Goat Victims and Other Assorted Trolls

Miniscule meandering
Shaping shortsighted ideas
Trapped in a tiny mind
Atrophied from long disuse
Smothered in the smug stench of arrogance
Dripping from every calloused thought
Bouncing through narrow mental caverns
Spilling forth in venomous sentences
Streaking across digital surfaces
Framed in spiteful paragraphs
Aiming to decimate hearts
And pulverize identities
Built through blood and sweat

All of that poisonous bravado
That swollen hollow ego
Shallow and decrepit
Serves only to hide the smallest coward
Too afraid of shadows
To bother with the light

Prompt: Selfish Love

<u>One More Thing Misunderstood</u>

Never thought to see another solo sunrise
Crack the sky with luminescent waves
Revealing only empty space
Where the curve of your form once embraced

No…there weren't supposed to be
Any other solitary exploits
On this planetary journey
Hurtling around the sun
No more lonely lunar escapades
Not one

Yes…this love is selfish
And I profess so freely
For when I asked you to be mine
I meant for all time

Life or Death be damned

Prompt: Ignorant

Self-Realization and Other Topics to Avoid

Information overload stuck on hyperdrive
Assaulting every sense I ever tried to maintain
Cramming bits and bytes into cranial cavities
Bursting from the mysteries unexplored
Unrenowned and otherwise unknown
And I try to imagine what it was before
Prior to this data center dungeon crawl
To dream of what it was to be ignorant
Of every passing philosophy

What I wouldn't give
To be young and dumb
Naïve and innocent
Again

Prompt: Lose Tides

It Happens Every Day and I'm on a Schedule

Startled in a quiet daze
Spun out silent in a winter rain
Watching Atlantic tides roll back
Swallowed by the incessant hunger
Of Mother Nature's lunar cycle

Losing every form they've ever known
Obliterated identity washed away
And pulled into the sanguine deep
Caught in Neptune's embrace

Seconds tick and fall away
Circling ageless solar dials
Building towards release
Pushed forth in violent exposition
Rebirth fully realized
Pounding in the saline surf

Prompt: Ocean

Roxanne and Other Red-Light Fables

Did you ever spend more than a moment
Lost in some sun sparkled daydream
That shimmered on the fringes
Or rippled with electric anticipation
And crackled in the swollen current?

It's funny…I never would have thought
To wonder all that long
On misplaced fairy tales
Or tired street corner clichés
But then I never caught eyes like these
Practiced vacancies
Staring laser beams
Hiding an ocean of imprisoned tears
And unspoken pleas
Sealed behind a calculated masquerade

That's when I lingered longer than a moment
And wondered what you dream of
In the secret hours
Far from the dark alleys
And shadowed shallow suitors

Prompt: Happiness

I Found the Rock 'n' Roll, What About the Rest?

Picked up that evening transmission
Modulated frequency floating in the subspace
Seeking out an open receiver
With mysterious intentions carefully entwined
In classic double entendrés
And melodies in reverse

It was always there
Slicing through the white noise
And all the crafted interference
Pulsing in subtle saccharine vibrations
Interstellar wavelengths
Delivered via binaural insertion

Click the knob
Turn it up
Maybe not quite to '11'
Let it overwhelm me
And cater happiness in every note

Time travel at its finest
In the form of Rock 'n' Roll enlightenment

Prompt: Galaxy

Yes, It Really is a Car

Rode the lens flare toward the ageless rim
Intently poised on the disappearing light
Slowly swallowed by the infinite increase
Expanding in the immeasurable depth
Of the yawning ebony singularity

Nothing escapes
Nothing survives

Gradually the realization rises
Abject horror dawning
In fits of animalistic terror
Cresting waves of isolation
Punctuated in the disintegrating atmosphere
With stolen gasps and silent screams

Stale popcorn casually flies
Breaking pent up tension
Laughing in the backseat of a Galaxy
Another Saturday night drive-in affair

Prompt: Understanding

Barely a Blip on the Radar

All these fractured puzzle pieces
Scattered in forgotten corners
Left to fade and peel away
Retaining cryptic imagery
Locked in asymmetrical angles
Barely noticed in the grand design

Oh…but the spark ignites
Flash bulb recognition
Burning silver flecks in glossy shine
Capturing that vanishing moment
In eternal soulless immortality
Frozen painlessly in vivid contrast
Tiny details etched in semi permanence
On crowded mental landscapes

Brilliance recognized
Emotion countersigned
Understanding never meant accepting
Or gave even the slightest hint
Of retreat or surrender

Prompt: Lost

Overflowing Streams of Consciousness

It's not enough sometimes to know the outcome
Won't match the total experience lived in between
These solar cycles spent in search of all the instances
I hardly though to keep track of and to hear it spill from the lips of others you might think I never lost a thing...never knew the pain
But I've lost...hope...faith...dignity...credibility...love...
25 pounds...that one girl's number I spent the whole night flirting to get...family...friends I barely knew...work...intimate strangers...WMDs...ideas...time...games...books...sleep...health ...flights...drinks...the only one I ever thought was going to be the one...even Life itself...

    Sure...I've lost...and everything that was ever worth anything
    Was waiting to be found...waiting for me to finally come around

Prompt: Missing Hearts

Scarecrow Brains and Other Things not in Kansas

Exhale

Let the swollen ego subside
And fade into the charcoal atmosphere
Hanging in the last frigid tendrils
Of winter's brittle grip

Inhale

Open your eyes to the possibility
Of more than just simply existing
On the fringes of spring's awakening

Breathe

Give this battered life
Another round of yellow brick wandering
Locating missing hearts
And time capsule courage

Just breathe for me

Prompt: Courage

Why is a Legitimate Question

Surely there has to be more to all of this
Than just the retread cliché analysis
Kept on speed dial
Spit out automated recall
Skimming surface effortless
And lacking any substance

Surely there has to be a different line of reason
Than just the force-fed establishment
Hanging on to empty traditions
And oppressive ideology

Surely this can't be all there is?

…and courage is birthed in the instant
You're not satisfied with the answer
'that's just the way it is…'

Prompt: Relationship

Isn't It What You Wished For?

If I promise to tell you every secret
And undo the veils of mystery
Will it prove to be enough to satisfy?

Is it knowledge that you're after?
With these rites and supplications
Bringing insomniac fits
And lethargic spells
Aiming for something
Worthy of the sell

Do you truly want to know?
Or is this only passing time?

The first one is free
But it costs everything

No relationship that survives
Is built on anything less
Than lifeblood and soul shards
In equal parts from as many sources

Prompt: Burning Flame

Yes, I Rubbed the Lamp

I don't know how long I lay there
Completely enveloped in ebony
And shrouded in aimless ignorance
Or what those concepts even meant
In the midst of such unending emptiness
That stretched to every corner
Of this limited experience
With the fragile nature of existence

Charred ozone left in the wake
Of an atmospheric discharge
Spreading thunderous tendrils
With blinding incision
Streaking outward
From a single burning flame
Interstellar epiphany awakening
In undisputed ecstasy

May be just for a moment
But I think I've died for less
And there's no corking the bottle now

Prompt: Lust

It's Still a Cage, even if You Can't See It

Passions simmering in secluded silence
Percolating tensions smolder and pop
Elevating surface temperatures
Flushing cheeks and trembling limbs
The sweetest taste of you recalled
Lingering on my lips
In a kiss I've never known
And I can almost feel your tempting touch
Gliding in electric euphoria
Until every fiber of flesh
Is screaming for the deepest union
Entwined in Aphrodite's sensual symphony
Enraptured by our consuming pleasure

And the dream ends
The playback stops
These fleeting moments spent
Feeding rabid ravenous dogs of lust
Leave me hollow and unsatisfied
Seeking more than just this ephemera

Prompt: The Enemy

The Sort of 'meh' Your Mother Warned You About

Going through every motion
Practiced disconnect
Echoing in staccato delay
That there is a kind of freedom in this display
Of habitual behavior is a lie easily believed
When we create monumental apathy
As some sort of trophy to obtain

Talking heads and pop psychologists
Proffer feel good "self-help"
Void of any actual discovery
That might have any lasting effect
On the collective cultural psyche
And somehow it's still always about "me"

Anxiety ratcheted to extremes
Fear set to threat level orange
With no indication of ever dropping off
And yet the ultimate enemy
Is not hounding the gate
It's enthroned in the hollow indifference
Plaguing the halls of our mentality

March Writing Challenge
March 2016

1. Respect
2. Thoughtful
3. Anger
4. Unwelcoming
5. Strangers
6. Wings
7. Sight Seeing
8. Paper Planes
9. Nocturnal
10. Spirits
11. Desperate
12. Enemies
13. Cold
14. Clouds
15. Texture
16. Family
17. Unworthy
18. Resentment
19. Closure
20. Missing
21. Colours
22. Baby
23. Broken
24. Satisfy
25. Forgotten
26. Myth
27. Love War
28. Planets
29. Feel
30. Beginnings
31. Endings

Prompt: Respect

...But Wait, There's More!

Subtle halflight spills into the archway
Warming weary limbs that shuffle slowly
Ambling towards a breakfast nook
And the wafting scent of Columbian divinity
Bubbling in the steaming pot

Reanimation in progress
As the first sip slides past welcoming lips
Lifting spirits
Stimulating mental faculties
In the sweetest measure

Flipping through the buzzworthy tidbits
On a flickering digital highway
New dates…old flames…someone's turned
Into a werewolf…and a personal ad screams
For your undivided attention
Claiming instant results
And the undying respect of your peers

Never knew respect could be bought
For only 3 easy payments of $39.95

Prompt: Thoughtful

Insert Desired Pop Song Reference Here

All those solitary evenings spent
Staring wide eyed at the rising moon
Wondering just where the little man lived
And how much green cheese there could
Possibly be in the wake of bovine athletics
Preceding runaway dishware
And the unspoken irony of a cat
Playing the fiddle

Everyone always seems to be telling you
Goodnight
In storied passages or amorous kisses
But I thought maybe you would rather hear
Hello

Prompt: Anger

Double Entendrés and the Rage of Heartbreak

There are moments when I have to question
What I'm even doing and if this path
Has any thriving purpose still building
In this seemingly endless vendetta
Born in the fires of annihilation

…but then I remember their vacant faces
And lifeless bodies piled in awkward stacks
My people cut down
Herded into unbridled extinction
At the hands of mechanical animals
Glitched and neurotic

…and that's when it ignites
The white-hot heat of anger
Boiling plasma
Bursting capillaries
Distilling every raw emotional shiv
Into the purest outpouring
Of irradiated holy rage

The universe will be held in conviction
No matter how much is left in ashes
Along the way

Prompt: Unwelcoming

Discotheque Delirium

There's a gleam balanced in the polished reflection
A subtle glint in those wandering eyes
And an absence of anything resembling restraint
It's not just a dance floor after all
It's a jungle!
A battlefield!
The hunting grounds!
Or some other terrible metaphor
For bad decisions
Drinks worth a mint
And the presence of inhuman predators
Stalking the weakest wills

Nothing more unwelcoming than conquest
And the smell of last night's desperation

Prompt: Strangers

Sleep is Overrated Here

Skimming jetstreams over twilight skies
Dipping through iridescence
In lazy looping pinwheels
Culminating in anxious runways
That swallow arriving airships
Delivering wide eyed initiates
To the always open arms
Of an insomniac apple island
Where there are no strangers
Only unknown friends
Seeking creative ways to exercise
Every sarcastic urge
Every bombastic dare
Floating off twisted tongues
Through cheeky grins
Rapid fire
With a wink and a nudge

Ya know what I mean?

Prompt: Wings

Illusions and New Arrivals

Inhaling the awakening scent of morning
Arriving with the breaking dawn
Sunlight peeking over distant hills
Invading the last foggy remnants
Of another moonless evening
Spent in contemplative slumber

Soft feathered wings break the silence
Beating against a biting breeze
Defying the urgent weight of gravity
And rising in purposed flight
Careening headlong into new days
And another chance at setting it right

Prompt: Sight Seeing

A Kind of Forgotten Magic

You were certainly the sight to see
Unleashed in utter abandon to the sound
The moment the first chord struck
Ringing in distorted staccato bursts
From overblown amplifiers
And electric cacophony

The ritual begins
The ceremony in review
Spinning circular pits
Crashing walls of death

Welcome to an average Friday night
At the palace of rock 'n' roll

Prompt: Paper Planes

Give Me a Minute, I'm Getting to the Good Part

Stirring soul breezes waft through
Unnamed hidden channels
Winding through spiritual recesses
That permeate my entire being

I am aware
If not completely sure
Of all these idle passengers
Clinging to honeyed words
That tumble from cunning lips
To test reactions and reassurances

It's a silly game
A sort of Pictionary pantomime
That lost my interest years ago
That left me sailing paper planes
From ivory towers
Neither of us ever did belong in

Prompt: Nocturnal

We're the Creatures…Well, you know…

Anticipation overwhelms the candid moments
As we watch the final solar shards
Disappear beyond event horizons
And eliminate the irradiated illumination
That dominates the daylight hours

All around
A collective inhalation occurs
In placid undertones
Cognition reawakening
With deliberate appeal rising
To greet the lunar wind
In such an ethereal fashion

We are nocturnal in every sense imaginable

Prompt: Spirits

Hanging About the Altar of Self-Incrimination

Clarity is such tricky business sometimes
Often fading from open view
Dancing between blurred lines
On foreign shores
And whispering sweet pleasures
In the midst of enigmatic hallucinations
Leaving me spent and undone
In the passing wake

I see it now
Though
Blossoming in undeniable hindsight
There are no spirits here
No wispy phantoms haunting
Witching hours
Just the ghost of your fleeting memory
Hanging in every hour gone

Prompt: Desperate

Allusions in Plain Sight

Desperate

Hanging on by slender silk tresses
Spun in silent symbiosis

Obvious

Dimestore pulp xenophobia
Masquerading in front page headlines

Parasite

Prompt: Enemies

All These Pieces on the Board

The tiniest infraction held fast
In miniscule microscopic detail
Imagining grievous slights
And unforgivable insults
That feign mortal wounds
In a jester's pride
Displayed with elephantine recall
And immortalized in hallowed texts
Unquestioned
Unexamined
Unilateral oblivion
Creating enemies in every interaction
Never leaving the gallows nest

Prompt: Cold

Ice Cubes Where a Heart Should Be

It was never about the standard overreaction
That permeated every conversation
You deigned to make yourself part of
Nor the self-serving allegations
Precision leveled in surgical attacks
To advance your Orwellian fabrications

No, such grandiose delusions
Are rather easy to dispel
In altruistic ruminations

It was your glacial touch
Trailing icepick talons
Down my shoulder blades
That finally did me in

Prompt: Clouds

The Island of Fallacy

A seaside shanty town left in sullen apathy
Softly sinking 'neath the weight of winter
Bursting with stubborn tenacity
And a crystalline powder drifting in fervor
Unabashed in tearing frozen clouds
From their darkened dreamless atmosphere

New Atlantis has arrived
Population: Unsurprised

Prompt: Texture

Marionettes and the Strings We Cut

All you managed to leave behind
Was the well-versed absence
Noted in your waning interaction
With any rationale
That didn't find its origin in you
Or some other greasy flattery
Whispered on twisted tongues
Leaving just the calloused texture
Of your Philistine conjecture

Like speaking braille in foreign accents
To a deaf audience of ventriloquists

Prompt: Family

Borrowing Lines and Stealing from Despair

Aimless wandering is an artform
Disguised as missed opportunities
And unfocused dreams in watercolor sunsets
That never quite align with all these expectations
Leveled in the hopes of well-intentioned family
Or misunderstanding friends projecting pop theology
In whatever flavor made the buzz list last night

If they only knew the freedom to be found
In take offs and landings on hidden shores
They'd drop every shackled moment
And catch the next flight anywhere

Prompt: Unworthy

Hamlet Meets the Cult of Personality

What did it feel like
Standing up on that elevated pedestal
Basking in their adulation
That fed your monumental ego
And overshadowed the humility you clung to
Once upon a time
In the earliest hours of a fabled history
No one bothered to record

I wonder
In those moments
Where you have yourself convinced
That you deserve all of this
Do you remember that small screaming fan
Buried within you bowing down
To some other legend
Shouting your unworthiness

Do you ever think you'll be him again
Or is the peasant really at the mercy
Of the emperor and his invisible coat
That beg for every scrap of attention
Anyone can give

Prompt: Resentment

Not the Kind of All-Nighter I've Been Hoping For

It's always in the early morning indigo
That the phantoms of overkill
Plague every exhausted thought
Trapped in this crowded headspace
Denying the relief of dreamless slumber

Neurotic self-obsession
Borderline resentment
Masked in humorless deprecation
Begging for any sort of release
From this imaginary prison
Bound for purgatorial shores

Never really did think much of insomnia before
And I damn well hate it now

Prompt: Closure

Afternoon Delight is a Bit of a Misnomer

Bursting skyrockets in tandem
Spiraling ever upward towards
Explosive inevitability
Locked into the supposed will of fate
That we might enjoy the briefest ecstasy
In our unanimous ascent into the heavens
Riding the friction to that ultimate climax…

…but there is little in the way of closure
To be found in the shower of sparks and ashes
That signal our remains
To the thunderous delight of every spectator
Waiting for the fall

Blade Runners and Electric Sheep

Flickering transmissions slip along
Digital jetstreams crackling with electronic impulses
That alternate in ones and zeroes
Coding binary heartbeats in missing pathways
Branching out towards artificial constructs
That simulate the complexity of our dichotomy
For definitive cognition
At the expense of any sense of mystery
That would bring exhilaration
And an undeniable reality
Experienced via virtual delivery
In the comfort of your own psyche

Prompt: Colours

It's Like Telephone but it Works

There was a dream once
Shared amongst the left out and forgotten
Whispered in hushed conversations
Hidden in the sheltered groves
On misty nights
In the hope of avoiding Medusa's glare
And the cost of Charon's fare

It could not be contained or silenced
Nor could the serpent overcome
Its undeniable appeal
With such fading hollow temptations

The blossoms spread like rainbow wildfire
Engulfing the valley in prismatic wonder
Giving sight to the colorblind
And the whispered dream is now a shout

Hope is never a vanity

Prompt: Baby

Off Script and Out of Lines Again

It always seems easier doesn't it
To just torch it all to cinders
And walk off through the smoking ruins
To play the "get out of empathy" free card
And toss the whole affair out
Through the bathroom window
Baby, water, and all
In such an awful cliché

Considering any other variation
Might mean some sort of admission
Of guilt or even feelings of remorse
And that simply doesn't fit within
This carefully constructed paradigm
Balanced on the knife edge
Of a disappearing grip on sanity
We're not sure was ever fully there

But then surety was never part of the deal

Prompt: Broken

On Any Given Sunday…Well, Maybe a Specific One…

It all seems like it started in a dream state
Full of flashback narrative
And hallucinogenic prophecy
Foretelling the miraculous arrival
Of a legitimate messiah

We tell ourselves any number of wild tales
And rationalize away the unexplained
To hide the broken emptiness
Threatening to swallow us whole
In microscopic doses

Moments pass
Clarity in the span of a thunderstrike
Enlightenment in an empty tomb
And a glorious resurrection

Prompt: Satisfy

__Believe Me, the Melody is that Good__

I thought I might be softly singing
'Satisfied Mind' in the afterglow
Of a transcendent encounter
Awash in the smoldering heat
Of a newly discovered passion
Enveloping the endless night

I never quite thought
I'd write a melody of my own
Undeniably enraptured
In your polyphonic embrace

Prompt: Forgotten

I Swear I Only Dozed for an Hour

Tiny dots flickering on the edges of the horizon
Spreading out in infinite directions
Until they're barely perceptible
Hardly distinguishable
Amalgamated into the formless chaos
Dancing on the fringes of eternal sunrise
And anything that might have recalled
A striking difference is long forgotten
In the twisting arms of multiversal galaxies
Spinning new threads and subtle stories
That bring the faintest déjà vu
With every animated telling
Around this dying campfire
Ushering in forever's slumber
At the gate called beautiful

Prompt: Myth

Strangled in A Minor

Suspected appetites swarm the recesses
Of an idle quarantine among the outer reaches
Of errant thoughts and empty dreams

I am all that's left of your better tomorrow
Suffocated by twisted ideology
Hunted like some mythical beast
To impending extinction
For some vain measure of control

When will you realize
That you'll never truly have me
Until you learn to let go?

Prompt: Love War

Fair Being a Relative Term...

I remember the sound of shells
Falling to earth with violent precision
Carrying the swollen might of furies
Hurtling toward their explosive destiny
With no capacity for remorse
Igniting fire blossoms on impact
Roaring the shared language of conflict

It's quiet now
Save for that tinny ringing bell
That refuses to be ignored
And motor functions that will not respond
While I lie here
Shattered and in so many pieces
Even Dr. Frankenstein
Wouldn't try to treat me
And all I can think of is her
And how I left her much the same

'All is fair in love and war...'
Such a bitter cliché
But savage in retrospection
If only I could avoid
Its haunting recollection

Prompt: Planets

Writing My Name with Solar Flair

Reflexes run rampant on the ramparts
Above the spiral pinnacles
Stabbing skyward toward the heavenlies
Like ancient archetypal compass points
Navigating galactic pathways
Leading to new discoveries
Unfolding in planetary enlightenment
At the speed of Renaissance typography
Spilled in slap dash heraldry
Among the frozen stars of Orion
Whispering granted wishes
In the arms of the Pleiades

Prompt: Feel

Behold the Field, Barren and Untended

Reaching deep within my innermost recesses
To locate the last shreds of empathy
Dangling by a dozen threads
In suspended subtle sufferings
Too miniscule to acknowledge
Without such deliberate meditation
On all that we never hoped to become
In the stunning absence
Of any sort of strategy
And left to stumble blindly
Through the tired motions
Of pretending to know
Exactly what it might be like
To feel anything ever again

Prompt: Beginnings

Somewhere Between the Harrowing and the Alchemy

Sparks in the ether
Tiny glimmering pinpoints
Arcing in the fading obsidian
Calling forth an age of mystic obsession
From the remains of infant ignorance
Long overdue for an upgrade
In the valley of the shadow
Of all that was ever expected
No matter how infuriatingly ridiculous
Or completely unrealistic

The first breath comes
Sharp and icy
In the gray blue dawn assault
On every virgin sense
Alive and receiving
Broadcasting overwhelming emotion
In this ever-lingering moment
Of sacred rebirth

Prompt: Endings

Ouroboros on the Outset of Dawn

Startled by the sudden arrhythmia
Of my heart's fascination
With unknown time signatures
And thrash metal tempos
In the quiet warmth of spring
That spreads in rapid electrical impulses
Flowing through extended limbs
In crashing violent surges
And my every thought consumed with
Last rites
Last regrets
Last wishes
Last will and testament
Passing crowded synapses
Overrun by blistered nerve endings
Screaming through seconds
Poised on the edge of oblivion
Knowing the finality
Is the moment of reckoning
And the serpent's tail
Has disappeared again

DNS Poetry August Challenge

August 2016

1. Long Distance Call
2. Dead in the Water
3. Bloodlust
4. Something Wicked
5. In My Time of Dying
6. No Exit
7. Bedtime Stories
8. Devil's Trap
9. Asylum
10. Time is on My Side
11. Yellow Fever
12. Sex and Violence
13. I'm No Angel
14. Wishful Thinking
15. Lucifer Rising
16. Let It Bleed
17. Abandon All Hope
18. Fallen Idols
19. Bad Seed
20. Paint It Black
21. Trial and Error
22. Goodbye Stranger
23. The Things We Left Behind
24. Sympathy for the Devil
25. Angel Heart
26. Torn and Frayed
27. Unforgiven
28. Two Minutes to Midnight
29. Changing Channels
30. Devil in the Details
31. Heaven Can't Wait
32. Rock and a Hard Place

Prompt: Long Distance Call

<u>A Light Left on and Other Myths</u>

The space between visits never mattered much
In the grand scheme of all we thought to be
Or hoped to mean to this developing paradigm
Enveloping the reality we tend to exist in

At least, that's what I wanted to believe

But the texts went unanswered
Emails unread
And there's only silence on the other end
Of another long-distance call
From the side of a stranger's bed

Guess there's more to absence
Than we care to admit
And the heart lost all its fondness
Somewhere between New York and nowhere

Prompt: Dead in the Water

The Other Side of a Tequila Sunrise

"Dead in the water"

I believe those were the exact words
That tumbled off your tongue
With the sort of vehemence reserved
For deposing politicians and charlatans
In the latest tell all exposé

I suppose it's not all that surprising
We never really meshed
Outside the realm of whiskey sunsets
And sweat soaked 5am regrets
All those sober interactions in between
Just ended with incendiary barbs
And increasingly awkward silences

Dead in the water?
Honey we never even left the dock

Prompt: Bloodlust

Can it Really be Torture if I Enjoy It?

The persistent metronomic drip
Of the antique shower head
Punctuating insomniac hours
Is enough to drive any man
To the teetering brink of madness

Have I already succumbed to the touch?

Staccato bursts soothing ragged nerves
Quieting a raging bloodlust
Boiling in swollen veins
Under a crimson moon

Am I already mad?

Prompt: Something Wicked

First Class, Head First, Straight Down

World weary sojourner in love's pursuit
Chasing lustful masquerades in half-hearted jest
Caught unaware in paper defenses

"Something wicked this way comes"
Breathing heathen temptations
For unlawful carnal knowledge
Burning through entwined limbs
Enraptured in the flames of forbidden bliss

Another satisfied casualty
On the voyage of the damned

Prompt: In My Time of Dying

Living Room Cherry Bombs and Bedroom Bottle Rockets

There were miniscule explosions
In the span between breaths
Indoor fireworks igniting
In the span between kisses
Destabilizing heartbeats
In capillary eruptions
Slowly draining vitality
With every inescapable embrace

If this be my time of dying
Then let it be known
You were always my favorite
Cardiac arrest

Prompt: No Exit

Thoughts on the Existence of Spoons

Impossibility

The kind of thought
Lost on the eternal optimist
Floating through life
On a wing and a prayer
To whatever might be out there
In the unknown realms

The ramifications cascade outward
Increasing waves washing past
In expanding magnitude
That warrant heightened attention

How freeing it must be
To see only opportunity
In this room without exits

Prompt: Bedtime Stories

<u>Looking for Boogeymen Between the Pages of Your Biography</u>

Did we ever for the faintest fleeting moment
Entertain the possibility
That all those fanciful bedtime stories
Spun to delight and tantalize our adolescence
In the twilight hours
Between bouts of sunshine
Might actually be real?
That all those bold adventures
And nightmare fueled horrors
May have roamed this fertile earth
In the decades distant past?

There, there…no need for undue alarm
Or insomnia anxiety
Just a few tall tales in the candlelight

No monsters dwell beneath this creaky bed…

Though the skeletons in the family closet
Are something else entirely…

Prompt: Devil's Trap

Manifest Destiny Trespassers will be Fed to the Army Ants

Sandpaper sunburn spreads
Blooming over parchment flesh
In rosy shades of violent red
The visible evidence
Of a trap laid by native devils
To dissuade foreign interlopers
From imperial pursuits

Saccharine stinging sensations
Slowly coursing through
Screaming rawhide nerves
As six-legged firebrands
creep and crawl

Devoured by glacial design

Prompt: Asylum

Hopscotch on Fire with Sheogorath

I never could quite determine the way back
From the blinding edge of madness
What with all the time spent skirting
The shoals off the coast
Of the shivering isles
In the grip of a saltwater delirium
And a vacation pleasure cruise
To the heart of a stolen enchantment
Encircling a wandering star

Too many overbearing stimuli
With no protection in sight

I sought only asylum
From these promontory predators
Ended up a permanent resident
With an ivory jacket

Prompt: Time is on My Side

Somewhere it's Me on that Beach in 'From Here to Eternity'

Amorous ashes scatter in the rising summer breeze
Fading remnants
Kindled intent
Cresting the waves of desire and indecision
Overthinking innocent affection
Wrapped in this warming embrace
Enthralled in the magic of her touch
And lost to the fleeting moment
Suspended in the eternal memory
Where time is ever on my side

Prompt: Yellow Fever

Missed Left Turns and Unfavorable Diagnoses

Wound up somewhere west of Omaha
Thumbing rides from passing truckers
Looking for the end of highway 30
Where I thought I might find a neo-fable
About a lonely stretch of sandy coastline
And the rolling indigo waves
Rushing in with salty kisses
And forever running away
It might just speak to my existence
Might even spark a hope or two

Doesn't really matter much
The highway stretches on
Eyes fixed on the cloudless blue
'cause if I pause for a reflection
A momentary recollection
I'll find myself wishing
For a Bugs Bunny piano drop
Or a double dose of scarlet yellow fever
Before I ever have to relive
That frozen instant
You burned the final bridges
Forever turned away

Prompt: Sex and Violence

They Tell Me it's Boring but They Just Can't Seem to Get Enough

Sex and violence on auto-response
To pacify the proletariat
And entice the bourgeoisie
Is this all there is to you?
Tired well-versed clichés
And predictable appeals
To animalistic pursuits
And primal urges?

If you really want to impress me
Try a little mental stimulation for a change
Make me crave your conversation
The challenge of your alliteration
Touch the deepest reaches within
From across the room
Bring me to the edge of ecstasy
On the wings of your philosophical bloom

Shatter this shallow reality

Prompt: I'm No Angel

Hypocrisy is not Exclusive, Anyone can Join…

It's amazing sometimes
How quickly these glass dwellers
Chuck stones at one another
Or feign surprise
When the circular firing squad
Leaves everyone bloody and bleating

I've never been much of an angel
Or laid claim to any such title
Though I am quite fond of this halo

Tinfoil, gold spray paint, and all

Looks just like that one you have
Balancing on those horns
You try so desperately to hide

Prompt: Wishful Thinking

It's 3am and Morpheus is Nowhere to be Found

Untended thoughts spill into the darkened hours
Roaming beyond the call of midnight
Mental gymnastics stretching behind exhausted eyes
Recalling every single scenario that might've been and never was
Neurons on overdrive despite the body's plea for rest
Insomnia breeding in the space between
Crippling anxiety and errant wishful thinking

Sleep is a foreign concept to the endless thought parade

Prompt: Lucifer Rising

But Speaking of Angels, You Know I was One Once Too…

I lived through all the ghosts of my former lives
Dreamed up these alternate endings for each and every one
Where I managed to somehow come out a hero
Despite all the satanic proclivities I swallowed down
Like the finest ambrosia in the palaces of Spring
Not quite unaware
More like unconcerned
With the gathering darkness 'til it was far too late
To prevent this spirit of Lucifer rising
In all the bastard morning glory it can muster
In the suffocating swell of pride
Seeking only complete control
Of all it can never have

…and the cycle continues while the ages flutter past
The bitter pill goes down
The defiance slowly burns
Delusion and metaphor the only scraps that remain…

Prompt: Let It Bleed

Dammit not this Myth Again...

The pulsating rhythms were hypnotic
Shuddering in alternating waves
Morse code metronome beating out this cry
Sudden exclamation ever strangely in time

Left the illusion of safe harbor ashore
To let the pages of this nightmare
Bleed among the terrors of the open sea
Amidst the haunting lullabies
Of Scylla and Charybdis

Prompt: Abandon All Hope

Wait, I Thought this Purgatory Place was a Town in Italy

Woke up in the arms of a violet haze
Hanging in the warm stale air
Of a backwater motel room
At the edge of this nameless town
That marked the end of another night
Fueled by whiskey and fading pickup lines
That must've worked by the sound
Of the body stirring beside me

Eyes flicker and adjust to the hidden light
Filtering in through venetian slits
Tilting in every direction
In this place that hope abandoned ages ago
And left to its own devices
Among the denizens of an imagination
Stuck in the throes of purgatorial angst
And I'm left to wonder if this is the part
Where the narrator chimes in
Or if I finally lost the plot for good

Prompt: Fallen Idols

How Did I Not See This Coming?

The implications were staggering
And not the sort of thing you just ignore
Like an errant word or a careless phrase
But the kind of realization
That thunders in reverberating shockwaves
And echoes deep within your very core

Mark your calendars
It was this day
That all these hollow empty idols
Lay fallen and discarded
Deaf to all the desperation
Mute and unknowing
In the face of impending apocalypse

The one thing never expected
At the end of the world party

Prompt: Bad Seed

It's Not Like a Summer in Mirkwood

What tends to be most fascinating
About the state of our humanity
Is just how quickly we want to point out
Some type of obscurity
Or existential excuse
To explain away the depravity
On full display

Just a bad seed
Born under a bad sign
In the bowels of some forgotten curse
As the seventh son
With lycanthropic porphyria
Enslaved to the wheel of fate

Heaven forbid we expect any sort
Of personal responsibility

That's just crazy talk

Prompt: Paint It Black

Might Not Have His Moves, But I Can Spout His Words

Found it buried in the irony
The somewhat subtle normalcy
Bouncing in between the sharpened extremes
Of unrestrained madness and dignified reason
Like some arrogant air hockey puck
Skipping into calculated violence
At the adversarial hands of fate

What does that really even mean anyway?
Normalcy? For who exactly?
Is it really worth the constant barrage
And expanded bruising?

Might be better to just paint it all
In varying shades of black
And disappear into the waiting shadows
That frame this fabled endless night

Prompt: Trial and Error

Quick isn't on the List Either...

Repetition feels like a vain pursuit
In the midst of asphyxiating frustrations
That seem to rear their hydra heads
Far too often for any level of comfort
And without much concern for eroding sanity

Still...what other choice can there be?
Sit here and wait for the blackout?
Give in to the cattle call?

It's just a day at a time routine
That slips between the knife
And the whetstone of progress
But there's no failure to be found
In the wake of all this trial and error
Only experience and possibility

No one ever said growth wasn't scathing

Prompt: Goodbye Stranger

More Sap than a Bleeding Maple Tree

Spent all weekend trying to decipher
The stolen secret languages
Buried in the aimless conversations
That punctuated cautious interactions
In our awkward amorous adventures

Is there a Rosetta stone hidden somewhere
With all the hieroglyphic enlightenment
Needed to unravel your captivating mystery?

Because I want nothing more than to say

Goodbye stranger
Hello lover

Welcome to the rest of our lives

Prompt: The Things We Left Behind

You're not Much of a Riddle When You Lay it All Out There

Dandelion fluff floating in the breeze
An entire existence terminated
In the violence of a gentle breath
Providing a predestined catalyst
In the wild light of germination
Leaving only empty stalks
Still heady with the hope of future birth

So too these vacant ruins
The silent things we left behind
Conversing only in archeology
And Homerian soliloquy
Communing in the passing wake
Producing more puzzling enigmas
Than this octogenarian sphinx
And avoiding anything resembling an answer
For another eon or two

Prompt: Sympathy for the Devil

We're Far Beyond 'Pleased to Meet You' at This Point...

It takes a special breed of audacity
For you to slither in here uninvited
And plead your case in shades
Of a victim's black and blue
As if you'd somehow been abused
Or coerced into chains

Such a striking change in tone
Quite the face you've drawn upon
I seem to recall a more accusatory bite
In the opening remarks
You hurled like lawn darts
At unsuspecting patrons
Attending the weirdest party
This side of the oncoming apocalypse

No...we all know your name by now Diablo
You'll find no sympathy here

Prompt: Angel Heart

__Verbal Arsonist Swallows Extinguisher Whole__

The concept of what might constitute an apology
Never saw the blazing daylight
Or even crossed my over-anxious mind
'til it was all too far gone
To stop your angel heart from bleeding out
From the "death by a thousand cuts"
Inflicted over countless careless arguments
And every cruel verbal barb
Delivered with all the thought
Of a newborn mayfly

I wanted to believe my greatest sins
Were something lofty and decadent
Worthy of Lucifer himself

…but nothing compares to the disappearing woman
Buried under a lifetime of redirected insecurity
And suffocating indifference

Prompt: Torn and Frayed

All the Things We Never Thought to Find

Dust sprites flutter in the stale attic air
Stirred by solo adventures in shadowplay
While searching out genealogical artifacts
And forgotten hallmarks of adolescence

Scattered boxes stacked in Jenga towers
Lining stilted walls
Holding untold secrets and unsent letters
Yellowed, torn, and fraying
In perfume scented envelopes
Recalling unspoken dreams
Washed out in the warm summer rains
And left to the passage of memory

Prompt: Unforgiven

I Made This Voodoo Doll of Myself to Maim You

Like a slow-motion car crash
Fast forward rewind on a permanent loop
I just can't look away
No matter the horror that awaits

You sat there seething in quiet rage
Memorizing a litany of the unforgiven
Swallowing down such poisonous bile
Never realizing the disintegration cover
Spread so tightly over your existence

I tried to empathize
Crawled through hot coals and broken glass
To demonstrate a measure of compassion
Long since dead in your eyes
And in the final act
You drank the rot prepared for the damned
Crushed beneath the weight
Of this self-inflicted martyrdom

Prompt: Two Minutes to Midnight

Iron Maidens in the Hands of Rocket Queens

It just never seemed to make the surface
That nagging sense of self-preservation
Designed to trigger warning signs
Long before the onrushing tidal wave
Threatened a shipwrecked existence
Balanced on the swinging pendulum
Two minutes from midnight
And the coronation of another fool's errand
In the grasp of the silent hours
Lost to the new moon absence
And the rolling fog of indifference

Prompt: Changing Channels

The Highway isn't Lost…I Just Misplaced It…

Empty miles of fractured asphalt
Stretch out in the pale illumination
Of yellowed headlights
Hypnotizing exhausted eyes chasing blurry lines
Invoking a lengthy yawn and clicking jaw
While surfing pirated airwaves
Looking for that one particular song
To extinguish the midnight monotony
And demolish the roadtrip doldrums

The beat slowly rises in warbling waves
Echoing the shimmering guitars
In a steady ½ time
With a plaintive observation
'I just don't miss you anymore'
And I wonder which one of us
Never saw that coming…

Prompt: Devil in the Details

Something About White Picket Fences and 2.5 Children

Scintillating suburbia spiraling slowly
In an altogether awkward descent
Drifting in between lazy Sunday picnics
And screaming Monday rush hour gridlock
Seeking precious equilibrium
Finding only the pitched grip of vertigo
Tugging on these ragged kite strings
Like some garish marionette
Unwinding devilish plot devices
Dangling in the smallest details
That read in lines of broken prose
Describing the world's last night
And other grand illusions
Left to court the vanishing sun
And revealing a master of none

Prompt: Heaven Can't Wait

If You Don't Stop to Look Around You Might Miss It

Just one moment
A single instance shining in the bright
That beckons to the weary dreamers
Glowing in the golden aura that hums
Familiar melodies in major keys
Soothing away the sandpaper sting
Of backwater anxiety

A solitary moment
Unique and light years from alone
In the rising chorus of the multitudes
Basking in glorious revelation
And laughing merrily at the notion
Of Heaven's Kingdom waiting for any man

No need to linger any longer
Loitering at the beautiful gate
Heaven is here

Prompt: Rock and a Hard Place

What Did You Think Proverbial Meant Exactly?

Staring down storied indecision
The kind of monumental choices
Worthy of a dozen labors
Inside the volcanic remnants
Of last week's fabled mistakes
With smoldering embers still smoking
In the near indescribable carnage
Of another game of existential chicken
Between the mythical rock and a hard place
With the very fabric of reality
Dangling tenuously in the balance

…but seriously do you want fries with that?

DNS Poetry September Challenge

September 2016

1. The Inefficiency of Emotion *(Grade)*
2. They Don't Make 'em Like They Used To *(Will Hoge)*
3. Black *(Pearl Jam)*
4. Sittin' Here *(Doop and the Inside Outlaws)*
5. The Taste of Ink *(The Used)*
6. Best Bad Girl *(Katie Grace)*
7. You're So Last Summer *(Taking Back Sunday)*
8. What a Shame *(Shinedown)*
9. The Only Exception *(Paramore)*
10. Good Time to Change *(Brandon Calhoon)*
11. Into the Airwaves *(Jack's Mannequin)*
12. I Just Might *(Sonia Leigh)*
13. Must've Run All Day *(Glassjaw)*
14. Living the Dream *(Sturgill Simpson)*
15. You Make My Dreams *(Hall & Oates)*
16. Somewhere in the Middle *(Cody Jinks)*
17. Here's to Us *(Halestorm)*
18. Wishing *(Sugarland)*
19. Make the Kill *(Elise Davis)*
20. Pretty Things *(Tony Lucca)*
21. A Story About a Girl *(Our Lady Peace)*
22. Day That I Die *(Zac Brown Band)*
23. Madness *(Muse)*
24. Sometimes I Cry *(Chris Stapleton)*
25. Caught *(Florence and the Machine)*
26. I've Been Loving You Too Long *(Otis Redding)*
27. Burned Me Out *(Honey Honey)*
28. Love Song *(Miranda Lambert)*
29. A New Hope *(Blink-182)*
30. That's Why I Write Songs *(Jamey Johnson)*

Prompt: The Inefficiency of Emotion

I Liked You Better Before You Left the Garage

This reaction is really nothing new
In the grand design of our checkered history
We circle around like spinning tops in combat
Succumbing to mosh pit politics
And scene kid hipster bullshit
Annotated like footnotes never referenced
But that's never stopped us
From holding on to this inflated self-importance
That we somehow claim for humility
Contradiction being standard
In this inefficient expression of emotion

It's hard to find the strength to care
In the sway of this empathetic deficiency
And I'd like to think you might feel differently
But you stopped considering anything
Remotely outside yourself

Prompt: They Don't Make 'em Like They Used To

Next You'll Tell Me the Good Things Were Never Meant to Last…

Smoke from the flat top drifted skyward
Caught in the hum of the overhead fan
As grease sizzles and pops off the charring beef
Delivered via after-hours menu
In this dilapidated truck stop westbound on 66

Rubbed my heavy eyes
Steam tendrils tickling my nose
Proof the coffee is hot
Not good…but hot
Attention drawn to a worn-out photograph
Snapshot of a faded era lost to the spilling sand

"They don't make 'em like they used to"
A consolation phrase on the lips of a cynical cook
Looking bored and strung out…jonesing for a cigarette

Everything seems to be better in the arms of the past
With an uncertain future and an imminent end

Prompt: Black

Eddie I Think I Might Know What You Meant

The fade in tends to catch me
Off guard and out of key
Searching for the pitch
That just rolls naturally
Dripping from every word
Escaping from your tongue
Inviting such complete adoration
Even though such moments
Are merely echoes
Ephemeral fragments
Faded love songs

All the memories are slipping away
Painted and tattooed
Washed in blackout tones
You're the center of someone else's universe
The sun and stars in their burning sky

I only ever wanted it to be mine

Prompt: Sittin' Here

I've got a lot on My Mind and You've got the Time

You might think it would just be customary
A sort of accepted social convention
Presupposed and obligatory
The kind of thing that's queued up and waiting
For another weekend curtain call
Filled with half-light and late nights
On the neverending whiskey crawl

Yet with all those surface festivities
I still seem to find myself underwhelmed
Sittin' here rocking a familiar barstool
Wondering if that's really all there is
In an alcohol fueled existentialist crisis
And looking for just the right moment
To disappear into the arms of a roadhouse angel
And another night of ecstatic amnesia
Trailed only by recollection and regret

Prompt: The Taste of Ink

Someone Took My Pound of Flesh a Long Time Ago

It's a vague attempt at supplication
Though some might say misdirection
Like a half-assed parlour trick
Or a charlatan's gambit

There's a bristling air of anticipation
Electric swell in charismatic idealization
Inspiring masochistic initiates
And mentally ravaged acolytes
Thirsting for the taste of blood and ink
In compulsory burnt offerings

Surprise is the default reaction
Suspended disbelief in full retraction
And somehow we always seemed to expect
A different outcome from these silent idols
Crafted in our own image
Built from our own consuming pride
Drowning in the same fathomless sea

Prompt: Best Bad Girl

The Whitest Lies have the Blackest Consequences

We try so hard in the deepest nocturnal hours
To convince ourselves that it's only this once
Only a momentary lapse in the strength we pretend

Surely this can be overlooked
Not even worth a mention
Or striking pen to paper

But I know
Oh, I know

You're just the lady of the evening
The best bad girl available in the heat of it all
A willing substitute for that elusive something
I've convinced myself I can never have

Cheap hangovers and expensive regrets
The inevitable price of settling for less

Prompt: You're So Last Summer

Aces and Eights Again

Clarity tends to set itself upon us
In the moments we don't really expect
Blinding us with the inescapable truths
We work so hard to push down into the dark
And bury beneath the idle fantasies
That suit this paradigm

No sense to be found in denying this now
No feelings left to wound or even be found
You're so last summer
And I'm a dream that's yet to occur
With no reasons left to wonder
Just when or why we never worked

Admission taps the wellspring
Let the river burst and wash me clean

Prompt: What a Shame

The Light is On and I'm Always Home

Solitary summer evening skies
Awash in tones of golden ochre
And buzzing with the patient hum of cicadas
Eliminating any chance of silent reflection
In a white noise lullaby
Welcoming the deepening night

It's a somewhat semi-lucid affair
Swinging in a borrowed backyard hammock
Drifting towards a down tempo dream
And a subconscious clarion call

What a shame this only ever happens
In the moments when you've left for all points
Between nowhere and never was

A shame it's all just in my head

Prompt: The Only Exception

Five Cent Psychiatry and the Doctor is In

It's an endless source of amusement
Ironic and unintentional
This comedy of errors that navigates en masse
As I carefully construct impermeable boundaries
And nonsensical guidelines
Meant to shape every unthought interaction
Manipulate each conversation
Towards some grand delusion
Where my world isn't crumbling
Like washed out seashore sandcastle ruins
And everybody loves me…laughs with me…
Plastic soul hypocrisy

You were the only exception
Brightest star in the black
Lighthouse of reality in my farcical sea

The only one that ever truly saw me for me

Prompt: Good Time to Change

I'm still Dreaming so I Know it's not Time Yet

Reflection
Precursor to interpretation
As to what it might really mean
In this broken moment
At the end of a road most traveled
Despite how unique we may want it to be

Am I reaching inward for enlightenment
Or just staring in the mirror?

Am I on the edge of eureka
Or just remembering a Blind Melon tune?

The man staring back at me laughs
Like I do in this case study absurd

Doesn't matter how you got here
Knowing it's a good time to change
Is the proof of growth
We're so desperately seeking

Prompt: Into the Airwaves

What You Thought was a Joyride was Just Me Escaping Again

Answers are often left unresolved
Despite the seeming urgency
To draw upon the certainty of closure
They're just left hanging there in the ether

Unbidden
Unasked for
Unremarkable

An apologetic sigh exhaled in resignation
Accompanies the interstellar transmission
Floating out into the airwaves via satellite
Wondering what they'll make of us
And the answers in the questions we found
So underwhelmingly unappealing

But Really, Where's the Fun in Sanity?

I think maybe you just assumed too much
About exactly what it is you represented
And the level of importance or esteem
You commanded in their midst

That's the trouble with ego really
Always so full of a smug sense of idealization
And an immortality complex
Even Mephistopheles never dared to dream of

The longer I watch this B-Movie horror show
You're so intent on bringing to life
The more I wonder if I just might
Have to let go of the sanity
You've clearly left behind

Prompt: Must've Run All Day

Electric Sheep Bleating Your Favorite Lullaby

Contrary to popular opinion
A kind of phrase designed to misdirect
In the guise of impromptu enlightenment
The sort of machination that must've run all day
Like a seditious advertising campaign
Banking on undiscovered propaganda
Living out a dream of postmodern suburbia
In the grip of a picket fence time capsule
With all the warmth of a cryogenic graveyard

Shhh…back to sleep my darling denizens…

We now return you to your program already in progress

Prompt: Living the Dream

Wake Me Up Before December Ends

The heart of September sauntered in
Ambling through the daylight hours
Without direction or hurry
Slowly savoring the subtlety
So often overlooked in the maniacal race
We tend to subjugate ourselves to
Out of ignorance or vanity
Who can say?

The pulse trickles forward
Steady rhythm in the atmosphere
Living out the dream we deny
No matter the lip service paid
And we surrender to the seduction of autumn
In all its temporal duality

Prompt: You Make My Dreams

Building on the Hopes of Infants

Glimmering cherubim board a gilded carousel
Bound in lazy cotton candy circles
Rotating endlessly in a calliope concerto
Where the golden clouds shed no tears
And the bubbling brook giggles in tiny rivulets
Dripping through verdant magnolia trees

You make my dreams a technicolor wonderland
Every time I close my eyes
In the afterglow of your innocence

Prompt: Somewhere in the Middle

All Things Considered, Strange to Mundane

Early morning silence hangs brightly
Permeating the edges of this soft illumination
Meant for aromatic coffee and contemplation
Of these existence-defining moments
Caught somewhere in the middle
Between a soaring delectable euphoria
And the plummeting upside-down dementia

Prompt: Here's to Us

__Drowning in all the Saccharine Sentiment__

It's the subtle quiet things
Small
Hardly noticed
All those little nuances
That result in goofy smiles
Silly laughter
And a soothing warmth unmatched
Undeniable
Unforgettable

Here's to us
And all the days yet to come
But mostly you
And all the dreams you've made true

Prompt: Wishing

It's not Surfing without a Board

I closed my eyes in the shuddering descent
Leaving only the engulfing pressure
Pounding out its unwavering crescendo
In the crowded space between my temples
That was overwhelmed until recently
With only thoughts of you and what you cling to
In the deepest connections sewn up in daydreams
And idle fantasies yet to be explored
Now drifting out into the arms of nevermore

Washed up in a Montauk wreckage
Wishing for some sign of vitality
But the signal returns without direction
And this station is non-operational

Prompt: Make the Kill

Snowblind Under Glass

There's a voice that surfaces in the deep
Rising in a kind of sinister incantation
That bleeds into the hollow verse
Recited ad infinitum in the aberration
Left unchecked and unrestrained
Until the madness sets in
And it's far too late to make the kill
And all that remains is unbridled heresy
In this hour of bloody insurrection

Prompt: Pretty Things

If I Knew The Answer We Wouldn't Be Here

Tiny spots bleed into my vision
Swimming out of a solar stare down
Meant to prove some sort of commitment

To what remains to be seen

Temporary blindness serves to hide
All those pretty things you masquerade in
Leaving only the quiet truths
So desperately avoided

Prompt: A Story About a Girl

All the Sub-Plots in Second Glances

All the clever lines tumbling free
Spinning out of their careful confines
And flowering in rapid anticipation
Of a bloom or bulb that brings epiphany
In the words hardly spoken aloud
Or to another
Despite the combustion of desire
In whiskey dreams and stolen scenes
From these nights in a rock 'n' roll haze

What's really left to say?
It's always been a story about a girl
And if you missed it
You haven't been paying attention

Prompt: Day that I Die

I Told You not to Step on That Butterfly

Little fissures slowly spread
Lining the surface in a tangled weave
Of wrinkles and canyons far from grand
But no less expansive
In the desert blaze that bleached this valley
In solitary eons past
Long before the flood
And well into the age of men now forgotten
In the swirling temporal sands
That fill this glass contraption
Never ceasing to be still…

…until that inopportune moment
Some careless traveler cracked the mystery
And split space and time in waves
That fractured galaxies
And erased a microverse
In an attempt to rewrite personal history
In the form of a single bullet theory

I am Time Immemorial
And this is the day I die

Prompt: Madness

Once More, Feeling or Otherwise

Seeds swiftly scatter
Stirred in the autumn breeze
And blown about like discarded chaff
In the harvest aftermath

Tumbling almost aimlessly
Bouncing into earthen pockmarks
And laid to rest in no less a tomb
Than the towering pyramids of ages past
To slumber in the madness of death unbound
To the confines of temporal progression
Awaiting rebirth and transformation
In the first light of spring

Prompt: Sometimes I Cry

It's Only a Theory Until Someone Loses an Eye

Steps and numbers fill the lines
Reveal just how much I cling to a perception
Of order in the broadest sense
And sometimes I cry out of desperation
Or imagined withheld revelation
Obscuring the natural selections
That lead me headlong into a realm
Defying classifications

You are the unbridled chaos
Passionate and raw
Antithetical and captivating
Stealing every quickening heartbeat
Leaving me truly terrified
And hung on every word

Prompt: Caught

Rejection is really a Matter of Perspective

Tried to capture your lightning in a bottle
Contain your essence in a bell jar
Like some coveted vanity trophy

I spent countless hours
Designing the perfect snare
Refining the ideal conversation
Meant to supersede defenses
And leave your heart bare

The effort can't be denied
Or overstated
But all I caught in the execution
Was the coldest shoulder
And a first-class invitation
To a long walk and a short pier

Prompt: I've Been Loving You Too Long

There's Never an Angry Sundown Worth Holding on To

That old door rattled on the hinges
Slamming accent to a pointed conversation
Now punctuated in the silence
Left hanging in your absence
While the heat slowly dissipates
And hindsight breeds clarity

Can't help but shake my head and smile
That rueful kinda smile
Found in the midst of a humble pie lunch
Served with a heaping pile of crow

Too much blood between us
To ever give up
I've been loving you far too long
To ever dream of letting go

Prompt: Burned Me Out

Something like a Restart or Maybe Just a Mulligan

The light danced out there on the horizon
Skirting the invisible line
Tightrope walking land to sky
In an effort to finally find that place
Where the two become one
Unified
Glorified
Burning every last part of me out
In a cleansing purge
And leaving an empty vessel
Waiting to be refilled

Prompt: Love Song

Those aren't the Songs on my Radio Tonight

Shine a light in the mental fog
Watch that smoky haze disappear
In the onset of clarity
That reveals a connection fathoms deep
And stronger than appearances would show
What you might call a silly love song
Means everything in their paradigm
And it speaks untold volumes
Dedicated to the discipline and devotion
Of the endless vows we only meet in dreams

Prompt: A New Hope

What, You Thought This Was Easy?

I wanted to find that great revelation
That sparkling moment of epiphany
Glimmering in the deepest shadows
Simply waiting for a patient discovery
At the hands of some charming rogue
Bent on delivering the latest and greatest
To all the awestruck masses
Ready to bestow thunderous praises
For the shiny new hope on full display
And ready for consumption…

Amazing how such a beautiful desire
Quickly becomes and ego driven monster

More amazing still
Just how badly my desire remains

Prompt: That's Why I Write Songs

It's Really Just Miscellaneous Goulash in the Making

Sloping slowly southward
Seeming somewhat salacious
Shared stoic steeplechase

That's why I write songs
An effort to disguise emotions
So readily apparent to everyone
In this moment of poignancy
Shared between strangers

Coral crystal constellations
Curving concentric caverns
Cling contented creations

Lost in the misread translation
Operating only on the feeling
Stolen signals flying blind
Alive in the exclamation
Pouring like wine from our lips

As Everything Turns Grey

November 2016

1. A Painting in Vengeance
2. The Debt for Happiness
3. The Natural Bridge
4. What We Reap
5. Late Night Vices
6. Purple is the Sky
7. The Taste of Time
8. The Problem with Temptation
9. All the Shaky Sounds
10. Reasons to Stay
11. Daisies in Winter
12. Pillow Talk
13. Eight Months After
14. Where We Hide Our Wild Things
15. Small Crimes Against You
16. All the Nameless
17. Maybe You Knew
18. Whitewashed Dreams
19. The Anatomy of a Wish
20. Planted in Pain
21. Heal to Tow
22. A House so Empty
23. Tell Me Where the Hope Lives
24. A Carnival of Heathens
25. Naked as the Name
26. Stumbling Over My Hallelujah
27. Soundless Downpours
28. A Fuse Too Short
29. No One Arrived
30. Sleeping with the Lights On

Prompt: A Painting in Vengeance

When it all Comes Crashing Down

An extracurricular affair
Built into the hangman's balance

A self-styled painting in vengeance
Left on display for the hoi polloi
Never far from the smell of scandal
Or the taste of blood and wine

No need to cite the sources
Our bias overshadows unspoken doubts
And reveals the preconceived pictures
We hold high with awkward pride

There's a noose in the oak tree
A mob just outside
Screaming about retribution
And God on their side

Prompt: The Debt for Happiness

Playing the Odds without Checking the Dice

It's cold here
Marooned in this frozen wasteland
Where winter is never in retreat
And the sun leaves only the palest light
To mark the path retread a thousand times
Maybe more

Am I simply resigned to this?
An aimless wanderer
Leaving bloody footprints in the snow?

The die was cast
A deal was struck
This is the debt for stolen happiness
And a life that was never mine

Prompt: The Natural Bridge

She says it's the Only Way to Fly

It's always in the unexpected alchemy
That subtle plot twist sewn beneath
The common threads of apparently
Mixed into the escalating tension
Between uninhibited vice and decency

Don't let that revelation stop you now
With all the misspent time and effort
On such gaudy display for the masses
Waiting for their evening fix
And permanently dope sick

You were looking for a natural bridge
Connecting the strands strung between
Ecstasy and Enlightenment

Never did quite get there
Now caught in the throes of addiction
And painfully self-aware

Prompt: What We Reap

Why Yes, it is Hotter in here since You Walked In

Dust rises from the barren flats
Floating in the arsonist breeze
Dry and hazy in the cloudless sky
Dominated by an irradiated star
Bathing the waking hours in abundance
That leaves even the proudest atheist
Praying for the smallest hint of rain

It's said you reap what you sow
Get what you give

Never been much of one for karma
But she hits like a brick
And you're just about as thick
With compassion on empty
And an overwhelming self-concern
That would make Narcissus blush

Prompt: Late Night Vices

Something about Logic and Reasoning Repeating Itself

Circles spin in undulating rhythms
Wearing grooves onto familiar tread
In the predictable fashion of time
Laid out in our linear diatribe
Dictating our fits of restless sleep
And full-blown waking interactivity
Punctuated by expected exhaustion
And the subtle swing of anxiety
That beckons all the late-night vices
With every hollow promise
Of an end to another lonely night
That's never truly realized
In the fleeting pleasures found here
And the circles continue to spin…

Prompt: Purple is the Sky

Violet Haze in My Mindscape

Thunderstruck in the awakening evening
Understanding dawning in a lightning strike
Illuminating hidden details
Unraveling the Rosetta stone mystery
That confounded silver centuries

Enlightenment spreads its wings
Rising into purple skies
Floating on hopes long deferred
And buried in the darkened traditions
Of "the way it's always been"

Truth unleashed in a wildfire
Scorching every last deceit

Prompt: The Taste of Time

When I Consider Everything Designed…

Staring up into the hazy morning sky
Afloat on the whims of reflection
Motionless and meditative
Emptying the tyranny of the urgent
Releasing the grip of anxiety
'til nothing remains in the present
But the taste of time suspended
And the absent sound of silence

I wait…and I listen…

Prompt: The Problem with Temptation

I Know it Happens to Everyone Else but I'm Different

It always seems so simple
Like it would be the easiest thing to do
To just reach out and take hold of desire
As if the wild-eyed storm would cease
Just for you in that moment
And everything would fall in line
Like the perfect domino parade
With no one the wiser
And everyone completely satisfied

That's the problem with temptation
Built on a source code of deception
With an allure of shaded innocence
And if you think you're immune
You're blindingly naïve

Prompt: All the Shaky Sounds

I Heard this Place is New Chernobyl

The playground relics creak and shudder
Turning slowly in the late-night breeze
Reliving all the former glories of summers past
Before the rust and decay overtook them
Before the nuclear winter arrived
And claimed this living valley
For the unending empire of the dead

No more children left to play here
The scorched flash mob murals
The only evidence there ever were
Replaced now by all the shaky sounds
Of insect reconnaissance
And evolutionary renaissance

We only wanted to live in peace
We only wanted to dream

Prompt: Reasons to Stay

Right on the Tip of My Tongue

It's that look
The one you gave me in that piercing moment
When everything just completely shattered
And fractured what felt like the core of us

I could see it in your eyes
Blue ones full of tears
Like Willie sang about
In the rain so long ago

I felt the sting in your kiss
Lips like ice and arsenic
Thought of a million reasons to say…stay

But none found a voice
'til long after you'd been gone

Prompt: Daisies in Winter

Seeds in Plain Sight

Quickened pulse streaming through
Filling a highway of throbbing veins
And arterial dimensions
Pushing into the wellspring of adrenaline surging
In the most heightened fashion
Leaving little to the overwrought imagination
But a few nagging doubts
And the oft forgotten promises deferred
Waiting past the fear of the present
Like daisies in winter
Buried beneath the mountain of ice
Germinating hibernation
Blessed by the first suns of Spring
And the endless possibilities of rebirth

Prompt: Pillow Talk

Conversations in Amber Afterthought

The evening solitude beckons softly
Calling out beneath the daily hustle
Reaching through the white noise
That seems ever present
And undetected
Yet completely domineering

Nightfall settles in
Indigo wings unfolding
And my thoughts spread into the quiet
Murmuring to the pillows beside me
Empty and undisturbed
It's the only conversation we have now
In the long years since you've gone

Prompt: Eight Months After

...and I don't even Feel like Singing...

Broke the lock on the gilded cage
Split the hinges in a daring escape
The first day you ever spoke my name
And offered another life to live out loud
Far from the shaded restraint of safety
The invisible shackles of normalcy
And the freedom to choose my own way
Within the realm of reach

Eight months slipped away
Mist in the dreaming I've retreated to
In the wake of your exit
And the shifting sands of empty promises

Inability to see the walls or the gate
Makes this ephemeral reality
No less a cage

Prompt: Where We Hide Our Wild Things

And the Oscar goes to…

Slipping into character
Discovering the roles we tend to play
The masks we tend to wear
Believing it a bravery in action
Facing the world when we can't face us
Suppressing the primal urge
To throw our heads back
And let the violent screams
Tear loose from ragged throats
Learning where we hide all those things
The wild and the untamed emotions
Compressed and imprisoned
Kept under the closest surveillance
Behind the smiling façade
Maintaining such glorious perfection

Can't keep the beast at bay forever
Sometimes it's best to play the joker
And let the cards fall as they may

Prompt: Small Crimes Against You

I Never Asked for Twenty/Twenty Anyway

Hindsight is such a burden
Portraying with sparkling clarity
All the pivotal moments
That shaped the stony path
We stumbled and fell upon
Recalling in vivid detail
All the small crimes of indifference
I committed against you
Weighed and measured
Piled up too high to ignore
That led to the demise
Of all we hoped to be

A burden and a teacher
Far too often ignored

Prompt: All the Nameless

This Shift is Murder

Stolen instruments of fevered desire
Signal the conflict between
The rational mind and impetuous heart
Both now lying in a shallow crevice
Unearthed among all these nameless graves
That cover the barren landscape
Stretching out
From the long-abandoned churchyard

Never dreamed this would be the end
Laid to rest in the potter's field
Between the soulless and the damned
But those the thirty silver coins
Slipped so readily through my fingers
And bought such a lovely shroud

Prompt: Maybe You Knew

Swimming Upstream in a Tsunami

It wasn't always something that came easy
The concept of surrender
A foreign notion in an era of ambition
And indomitable pride
I'll make it work by the skin of my teeth
And the bloody blisters on my hands
Success of my own making
Built on 52 cards and a sandcastle
And I think maybe you knew the secret
All the while you smiled
Let me suffer the collapse
And feel the weight of fragility

Epiphany unfolding in the reclamation
Surrender isn't giving in
It's knowing there's more to living
Than my own strength alone

Prompt: Whitewashed Dreams

<u>1984 Calling from the Clean Room on Phobos</u>

Blank walls encompass empty rooms
A misguided effort at tabula rasa
And whitewashed dreams
In the hope of some fabled new beginning
Full of pristine cleanliness
Sanitized and sterilized
Devoid of the unique and individual
Undergoing Stepford programming
With a promise of a place to belong
When you're just like everyone else

…and when everyone's the same
There will be no real humanity left
Just the pretty spent husks
Littering the polished floors
Consumed by their slavery to -isms
Impaled on the breaking dawn
Of their brave new world

Prompt: The Anatomy of a Wish

...and it Made no Difference Who You Were

The chill permeating the atmosphere
Was not the only frigid recompense
To be found in the indigo hours
That precede the eternal dawn
While stretched like some specimen
Meant only to serve idle curiosities

I am the dream you clung to
Dissect and vivisect
Searching for the anatomy of a wish
You sent out on falling stars
Plummeting earthward

I am the hope you now deny
In favor of "growing up"
And leaving fairy tales behind

Prompt: Planted in Pain

Golden Apples and Iron Bells

Thoughts in careless flight
Roaming the expanse of skies
That fill the edges of memory
Tempted towards the unknown horizon
And the wonder of the unexplored
Longing for answers to all these seeds of doubt
Planted in the pain of silence
And left at the mercy of understanding
That marches to its own time
Never quite in line with expectations

Still it's a sight to see
The harvest reaping
Electrical enlightenment unfolding
Answers rising undeterred
No matter the cost or the consequence

Prompt: Heal to Tow

Millstones and Other Gaudy Neckties

Strength is birthed within
Molded in the heat of adversity
And unrelenting determination
So often overshadowed by anxiety
And the constant nagging "what if"
That seeks to undermine every step
Toward the healing light of hope
And the severed ties of guilt
That we're shackled to and tow behind
The weight of self-importance

Strength is birthed within
Blossoming in the moment
We learn to let go and live

Prompt: A House so Empty

Charlie doesn't Swim Either

It sits there in silence now
Dilapidated and decaying slowly
Beneath the expanding coat of dust
Attracting only lonely ghosts
And termite reconstructionists
Looking for a fresh meal

What stories could it hold?
A house so empty now
Sinking back
Into the encroaching swamp
It once rose above
What secrets does it keep?
A home long since abandoned
Once filled with love and promise
Echoing only sadness
And the smell of napalm in the morning

Prompt: Tell Me where the Hope Lives

<u>Crashing the Existential Party Scene</u>

I've seen that place before
Walked through its fields and high places
Soaked in its warmth and radiance
Smiled & laughed in the house where hope lives

Seems like a dream now
Surrounded in the gloomy shroud I've accepted
Ensnared in this darkness
Masquerading as my reality

Still it flickers there in the distance
Off beyond the valley of insecurity
That runs between these twin peaks
Of deceit and despair

I feel it calling to me softly…intently…
That light that never goes out
And burns like a million supernova stars
In a peace without end

And I will get back there
I will get back there

Prompt: A Carnival of Heathens

Not Far From Thunderdome

Swollen bodies piled in the morning sun
The groaning sound of expiration rising
In a grim reminder of this endless war
That stretches ever on between us
For reasons long forgotten
A legacy bequeathed in bloodshed
And baptized in the tears of our grief

We wandered through the western wastelands
Searching for new lives to start
New loves to court
Only came across a dying carnival of heathens
Lost and completely self-absorbed
Offering cursory delights
For an unimaginable price

Nightfall settles
The stalkers howl
We yearn for sleep
Pray the Lord our souls to keep

Prompt: Naked as the Name

A World of an Oyster in tune with the Proclaimers

I think I must've walked for ages
A thousand miles or more in circles
Not really lost but probably not found
Naked as the name I was born with
Seeking the sort of purpose
That breeds clarity in a lunatic expression
Overwhelming and a little frightening
An ordinary evening in Bangkok
Staring down the empire of the sun

Prompt: Stumbling Over My Hallelujah

The Chorus and the Refrain

There are days when I can't seem to speak
Or even find the sounds necessary
To form the words and birth the phrases
That might somehow provide expression
For all the deepest longings
Welling up in this fountain heart
That wants to just erupt
And let it all fly in a dazzling torrent
Of emotion and adoration
Release the full extent of joy
That's been buried and denied

Sitting here tongue-tied
Stumbling over my hallelujah
Learning the secrets of silence
And the knowledge of remaining still

Prompt: Soundless Downpours

Made of Glass and Silver Sand

Caught out by surprise
Alone in the fury of a summer thunderstorm
Pounding the southern coastline
And I stand there drenched to the marrow
Screaming blue murder
To the blackened skies
Leveling challenges at imagined slights
Knee deep in the roiling surf

Then it hit me
Fast as…well…lightning
Electric streak lit up and surging
Rippling through every inch
Falling into the oncoming waves
Ears full of pumping blood
While the soundless downpour falls
Framing the cost of arrogance
And a funeral at sea

Prompt: A Fuse Too Short

Inventing New Personas a Quarter Stick at a Time

Silence and strange amusements
Precursors to the eventual eruption
That builds to an undeniable detonation
And buries us all in the caustic fires
Of razored retaliation
And the painful explosion
Of a fuse far too short
To ever allow any sort of growth
While living with single ply skin
And complaining that no one ever laughs
Or can seem to take a joke

A walking study in irony
Or a practiced hypocrisy

Prompt: No One Arrived

Spokes in the Wheel of Time and Space

Stayed up well past the point of exhaustion
Keeping watch or so I thought
Eyes on fire and crimson
Staring out over the stagnant horizon
Watching for signs of life
Expecting an imminent arrival
Friends
Comrades
Bitter rivals
Mortal enemies
Anyone

Anyone?

Eons trickled past
My bones still stationed sentry
Waiting for no one in particular

Prompt: Sleeping with the Lights On

Romancing the Bogeyman in the Closet

The smallest creaking floorboards
Shifting weight and settling foundation
Tiny timbers tapping on aging panes of glass
All the fuel required
Overactive imagination on overdrive
Devising elaborate scenarios
Hollywood horror clichés
1,001 ways to die in bed
While sleeping with the lights on
And no amount of reassurance
Yields the slightest release
There are still monsters in the closet
And demons in my head

December Falls Poetry Challenge
December 2016

1. Sinking Moon
2. Warm and Wild
3. Roasted Marshmallows
4. Impulsive Craving
5. Snowfall
6. Museum of My Heart
7. Serendipitous
8. Whiskey Nights
9. Midnight Dance
10. Deliberate
11. Fire in Her Soul
12. Holy
13. Dragonfly Heart
14. Love Languages
15. Toast to Us

Prompt: Sinking Moon

Weary in the Grasp of the Sea

I can still hear it in my head
The awful sound of twisted metal
Being strained and pulled apart
Shuddering and straining
Surrendering to the jaws of fate
And the swollen belly of the sea

We sat there watching
Huddled and shivering in lifeboats
With the sinking autumn moon
Illuminating the wreckage
Revealing the nature of our plight
And the condition of our hearts

It's dark now
And many days have past
I keep thinking the sun will rise
A rescue will come
But the air tastes like blood
And there's a frenzy
Just waiting to feed

Prompt: Warm and Wild

Sensory Smorgasbord Salutations

I caught the faintest scent of you
Spark of a memory
Subtle and seductive
Warm and wild on the southern breeze
The last gasp of autumn's serenade

I smiled at the recollection
An afternoon in the lost woods
Searching for a bit of solitude
Among the ancient sentinels
Laughing in each other's arms
Laid out beside a golden stream

Just a flicker between synapses
A click on the second hand
Felt like a glimpse of forever
Tasted of immortal eternity
Wouldn't trade it for anything

Prompt: Roasted Marshmallows

The Ties that Bind are Frayed not Broken

We always found a way
Despite the urgency of schedules
The demands of the everyday routine
To carve out the necessities
Of our meta-modern family
Like Saturday morning cartoons
Random holidays
Sunday night bonfires
Roasted marshmallows and all
Hot chocolate and board games
The Wednesday night charades
And even when the angst exploded
No doubts were ever entertained
On the love fully displayed

We always found a way
No reason to give up now

Prompt: Impulsive Cravings

<u>Voices and the Choices they Wield</u>

Irresistible suggestions slowly sink below
Permeating every waking thought
Coloring the process with shifting shades
That trigger impulsive cravings
Insatiable and unrelenting in pursuit
'til the last shred of will expires
And I'm left in the spent debris
Of all these fruitless decisions
Wondering just how many moments
Will be spent in remembrance of this one
And the taste of unwelcome deceit

Prompt: Snowfall

<u>Naked in the Blizzard's Breach</u>

Something shimmers in the distance
A faint echo of uniqueness
Amid the overwhelming uniformity
That drifts downward from the heavens
Blanketing the frozen earth in snowfall
Crisp white and wonderfully clean
Covering the multitude of barren scars
Left in the landscape
Evidence of our passing
Hallmarks of humankind
And the unknown still shimmers
Beckoning us out into the avalanche of night

Prompt: Museum of My Heart

Hands off the Exhibits and no Flash Photography

Eyes closed in the half light of dusk
Resting in the deepened chill
That precedes this winter arrival
And reflecting inward
On roads long past
Roads to come

Recollections rising
Stretching out in halls and chambers
Memories and regrets on full display
In this museum of the heart
Laid out with a audio tour
Video replay on repeat

Looking for the balance
Dangling between caution and impulse
Pressing into the wind
For the risk…the reward…
When everything around me
Is a screaming siren
and a five-alarm warning sign

Prompt: Serendipitous

Looking for Life in a Black Hole

Spiraling out of the arms of galaxies
Ever expanding in the emptiness
That envelopes light and sound
Traveling beyond speed without resistance
In the wake of enlightened consciousness
And a serendipitous encounter
Driven at the cost of thought unencumbered
By the weight of finite mortality

My mind is alive with a million stars
Each one a galaxy of its own
And a brilliant beacon
In another fold of eternity

Prompt: Whiskey Nights

Last Call and Other Warning Labels

Candles flicker in the stirring air
Wavering shafts of light
Invading solemn shadows
Spreading out in the forgotten corners
Of another empty motel room
That will serve these transient needs
In the dwindling hours
Of another night spent chasing answers
In the bottom of whisky bottles
That never knew the questions
And only offered a respite
From the labor of remembrance
'til the first crow of dawn sounds
And you welcome hazy recollections
And the throbbing ache of dehydration
And wonder if it will ever make sense
In the hours of sober reflection

Prompt: Midnight Dance

Freedom at the Expense of Delirium

Alight on the breeze drifting through sunset
Warm and inviting in the dying daylight
With just the subtle hint of unspoken desire
Tingling in the back of the imagination
Spinning elaborate hidden fantasies
Hanging just beyond the grasp of reality
Dancing in the arms of midnight
When dreams shine like supernovas
And I remember the taste of your name
Lilting off my tongue in the sweetest melody
Vanishing into the hungering night
And left homeless in the city of love

Prompt: Deliberate

Dinner Theater with the Hatfields and McCoys

Silence draped itself about the sullen room
Blanketing in layers over angled propositions
And you can feel the soaring tension
Straining at the bounds of common niceties
As we calculate and commiserate
Over every chosen turn of phrase
Weighing all these words and opinions
With such deliberate intentions
And all the while wondering
Who would be the first to crack
Unleashing total pandemonium

Prompt: Fire in Her Soul

It Was Only A Kiss...

It's sometimes hidden in the way
The light sparkles and dances in her eyes
The knowing glint
Mischievous and a little wild
Hinting at all the pent-up passion
Bubbling and percolating within

And when her fingertips find flesh
Tracing tiny circles
Tingling through your chest
Every hesitation evaporating
In the span of a bitten bottom lip

Can't remember when it ended
Overwhelmed in the euphoric flood
Enraptured in pleasures untold
Willful immolation
By the fire in her soul

Prompt: Holy

Something like Fire in the Sky

First snowfall of the evening glistening softly
Slowly floating out of frozen skies
Dusting all those empty streets in ivory
Clean and new under the rising solstice moon
We shiver out here in the open country
Far from the holiday bustling
Tending to these shepherds' flocks
Praying for a little warmth and a revolution

Startled in a holy vision
Surrounded by heaven's host
And a royal proclamation
Overcome in fearful reverence
And the taste of infant hope

What could this truly be?
Isn't it something to see?

Next stop Bethlehem, 0 A.D.

Prompt: Dragonfly Heart

Everything You Dreamed Was Real

Yellow skies and fading light
Last gasps of the course of day
Slowly yielding to the blossom of night
Unfolding in the starlit corners

Naked in the expanse
Intimate and unashamed
Dragonfly heart laid barer
To the taste of your knowledge

Luminary self-awareness
Softly spreading imagination
Washed clean of manipulation
Souls entwined in eternal creation

Prompt: Love Languages

The Machine has an Exit You can Find

Amazing is a word too easily employed
Amused by all those shallow minds
Starved for the smallest spark
Of imagination and wonderment
That set the skies of their youth ablaze

It's quite dark here now
The end result of every subtle slight
And conformities' undertow
That pulls them into the firing line
Like the drones they're shaped to be

Is it still there in your dreams?
The secret handshakes
And carefully constructed love languages
That used to fill our waking hours
And amplify our heartsongs

Or do they tell you
What to dream now too?

Prompt: Toast to Us

We're not all Dreaming of New Beginnings

Winding down in the afterglow
Final seconds of the ticking haze
Where we find it's precariously obscured
And painted over in solid minor chords
That tempt a dirge when a waltz would do
Where a man steps onto a folding chair
Proposing the last toast to us
And all we might've been
Which would be good for a laugh or two
If they only knew
We missed you last year
And an appearance in this one is as likely
As Atlantis off the coast of Wales

Mad March Poetry Challenge

(Inspired by Alice in Wonderland)

March 2017

1. Throwing Teacups
2. Down the Rabbit Hole
3. A Bottle Marked Poison
4. Painting Roses
5. Mad Hatter
6. Tea Party
7. Looking Glass
8. Off with Your Head
9. Chessboard Queen
10. It is My Crown
11. The Blood of the Jabberwocky
12. Evaporating Skills
13. A Crazy, Mad, Wonderful Idea
14. Six Impossible Things
15. The Smallest Door
16. Contrariwise
17. Nohow
18. Everything is Nonsense
19. Bandersnatch Eye
20. East to Queast
21. Futterwacken
22. Bloody Big Head
23. House of Cards
24. Flamingoes and Hedgehogs
25. You're Terribly Late
26. Muchness
27. Cheshire Grin
28. The Raven and the Writing Desk
29. Ticking Clock
30. Take Me to Wonderland
31. Fairfarren

Prompt: Throwing Teacups

I Think this Tea is from Long Island

Inspiration flickering in suspension
Dangling in the span between heartbeats
Spoiled muses dancing on a dinner table
Dashing teacups against the lattice frame
Of a dilapidated gazebo teetering in denial
Of dehydrated flower gardens dissolving
Crumbling under disappearing dimensions
Slowly lost in the darkened plot
Drifting out of emptied decanters
Drunk again and not a pen in sight

Prompt: Down the Rabbit Hole

Wait, was this the Red Pill?

Breeze rolling in off the eastern coast
Salt tinged and storm laden
Carrying your gilded tidings
With the barest hint of mischief
Tucked behind that twinkle in your eye
And it wasn't long before you found me
Camped out in the shaded speakeasy
Fading memory of a jukebox Romeo
Singing somber souls toward Sovengarde
And a light not easily dismissed

Never could resist that charm
Or that tempting smile…

Now we're tumbling down our rabbit hole
Wondering just how deep we go

Prompt: A Bottle Marked Poison

Avoiding Warning Labels

Fading ink on yellowed pages
Hallmarks of use spanning decades
Well-read and well-rehearsed
With no surprise in the delivery
And they repeat every line
Like liturgies in spring

Small wonder then
Passed out on the banks of the Rhine
Clutching a bottle marked poison
Mere feet from Aqua Vitale

Prompt: Painting Roses

Watercolor Florist On Demand

Wonder what thoughts spanned your mind
And gave birth to the suppositions declared
In the absence of rationality
Tell me truly
Was this really the outcome desired?
Did they promise an end
To the cacophony orchestrated out of key?

It is silent now
Beautiful painted roses
In the hands of skeletons
Released from closet tombs
In full view of your biggest fans

Prompt: Mad Hatter

Silver Highways and Minutemen

I told myself there was really nothing
To see here amidst the anarchy of emotion
That overwhelms the basic tenets prescribed
And laid out in common understanding
But like so many lies before
It was just too rational to be completely true
And carried a modicum of boredom
That could simply be endured no longer
When the party's raging around me
Like summer wildfires in full blaze
Waltzing with the Mad Hatter
While the March Hare plays a dirge
Drinking another round of high tea
Talking backwards and stabbing time
Exchanging madness like currency
Double nickels on the dime

Prompt: Tea Party

The Imagination is Always the First to Go...

It wasn't all that long ago
Sunny afternoons spanning summer days
Spent entertaining plush dignitaries
And diplomats from barbie kingdoms
At the most stylish tea parties
The fanciest imagination trips
To the edge of the unknown wild
And well beyond

Wasn't that far in the past
The memories still fresh
Yet it feels like some kind of dream
Only half real and fading in the bleed
Another casualty in coming of age

Prompt: Looking Glass

Adventures in Indigestion

Subtle shifts in the fabric of the bleed
Blurred at the edges of space unseen
And whispering into the void
Nestled deep within the looking glass
That holds the dim reflections
Of every nightmare called to mind
In the dead of time
Just waiting for an unsuspecting dreamer
To wish upon a screaming star
And unleash the modern specters
Upon the collective consciousness
Of the world's last night

No more chili dogs before bed…

Prompts: Off with Your Head/Chessboard Queen

Checkmate Guillotine in Full Effect

It's a curious game we've joined
Plotted in perpendicular lines
And alternating shades
Binary squares phasing propositions
Set in guided pathways
That breathe out measured gambits
To out maneuver the chessboard queen
Stalking the opposite end
With an erratic precision
And a delusional persuasion
Bleeding from imagined hearts
Screaming for instantaneous executions
And the rhythm of rolling heads

Prompts: It is My Crown/The Blood of the Jabberwocky

Heavy is the Head was Never so True Before Now

Eyelids flutter open
Batting back the invading light
Flooding into weary orbs
Begging for another hour of respite
From the weight of rule
That bends the necks of lesser men
Beneath the density of a crown
Bathed in the blood and fire
Of the monstrous Jabberwocky
And forged in the pit of Ulig's wrath
A living testament to violent nobility

…and I would trade it all for one more trip
On the never-ending sea…

I Was Really Doing My Best Whale Impression There

Safety nets swiftly cast away
Let loose into the death-defying main event
With all the raging arrogance
Of the crazy, maddening ideas in flight
Immortality imagined
Wonderful and terrifying
Stretching out through fingertips released
Watching the trapeze swing wide

…split second doubts flash by
Evaporating every skill ever possessed
And I make friends with the ground
In the worst way conceived

Prompts: Six Impossible Things/The Smallest Door

Needle Eyes and their Camel Companions

Golden dust glitters in the dusky half-light
Swirling in the breeze sweeping out of the north
Where the angry scars and fading dreams
Of yesterday are long remembered in songs
And bloody oaths on the tongue of every man
That speak of six impossible things
Five secret rings
Four corners of scattered earth
Three queens of royal birth
Two millennia shackled to the hounds of death
One key to reveal every hidden thing
And the smallest door we're shut behind
Guarded by dragons of fire and ice

Prompts: Contrariwise/Nohow

Spring-loaded and Tethered to an Apocalypse

Sparklers crisscross the summer air
Painting with evaporating illumination
And imagined sleight of hand
That plays on golden aspirations
Running contrariwise to every impulse
That springs from the darkened wellspring
Of a heart bathed in bloody notions
Screaming for undivided attention
To the smallest details of a life unbound
And a soul rising above it all
Hitching a ride on a skyrocket
Without ever looking back
No way…no how…

Flights of Fancy Under Glass

Folding paper cranes
Standing sand hill centerpiece
Speaking fluent liturgies
That frequent the tongues of sparrows
In flight on the southern breeze
Seeking warmer climes
And stranger times
Avoiding roving Bandersnatch eyes
Looking for avian souls to devour
In a land where everything is nonsense
And nothing is as it seems
The one-eyed jack is a mischief maker
Stealing royal tarts
And concealing winning aces
For a game no one knows we're playing

Something About Monkeys and Flying Butts

Silver sideways skylight serenade
Rapidly running rainy rivulets
Down dogged dispenser drains
Inside inexorable icy igloos
Featuring full futterwacken frivolity
Bared boldly beyond bravery
Cleft cautiously curiously crystalline
Portioned playful porcelain porcupine
Trees telling tall tales

Hard to get the words to fall in line
Traveling east to queast
Searching west to zelest
Dreaming of a single moment of clarity
And escaping at terminal velocity

Prompts: Bloody Big Head/House of Cards

A Full Deck was Never Even in the Picture

I imagined all of this
Unleashed the rabid hounds of production
For the most careful inspiration
To defy the hollow speculation
Displayed in the sneering ignorance
Of the heartiest detractors
Whispering their deceit
And I surpass every expectation
In spite of the measured detriment

…never did worry about foreign gambits
Triggered by jealous grifters
When the most dangerous saboteur
Dwells comfortably within
Precariously balancing a house of cards
Atop a bloody swollen big head
Deflated at the slightest damaged ego

Prompts: Flamingoes& Hedgehogs/You're Terribly Late

If it was Only a Dream, Why is there a Hedgehog in the Bed?

Spun out and sun drenched
Body sprawling across the summer sands spread eagle
Wondering how I got here on this nameless beach
Watching flamingoes and hedgehogs
Partnered in the strangest dance
Carrying them out across the glass dunes
And deep into the cotton candy waves
That flutter against the break
Spraying sugary foam
That leaves me dumbfounded and ridiculous

Eyes snap open
Cold digital noise fills the air
Another missed alarm
And the sweetest voice beside me
That whispers just how late I really am

Prompts: Muchness/Cheshire Grin

<u>We've All Been Touched By It After All…</u>

Forever in between
The overwhelming muchness
And the voracious nothingness
Both vying for total control

…and I just sit here
Sporting the biggest Cheshire grin
And wondering just what sort
Of madness inflicts us all

Mixing Metaphors Maniacally

Alarming artistry among acolytes
The kind sending spinal shivers skyward
At the mere thought
Alone in the deepening evening
Lost in the pages of a classic tale of terror
Feeling every creeping pulse
Of the tell-tale heart
And the ominous warning of the raven
That inspires countless hours at the writing desk
Looking for the same everlasting spark of genius
Listening to the rhythm of the ticking clock
Shuffling into the arms of immortality
Hastening the fall of the house of Usher

Prompts: Take Me to Wonderland/Fairfarren

We Were Legends Once

We set out in search of golden shores
Across the Venusian seas
First class ticket to an alien wonderland
Maiden voyage of the latent daydreamers
Cast off from the empire of the sun
Wishing fairfarren to all those we leave behind
Singing hopeful melodies
And promising a now long fabled return

About the Author/Contact Info

David Greshel is a Mississippi-born, Florida-bred author and poet with a penchant for music, movies, and all things pop culture. Never one to shy away from self-reflection and evaluation, he channels it all into his writing with the results you now see before you.

David currently resides in Palm Bay Florida and can often be found at live music events when not working, writing, or spending time with friends and family.

This is his third collection of poetry. His first two collections - Windows into the Past for the Camera Shy, and Nomads, Pilgrims, Troubadours - are also available everywhere.

Connect with David:

Email: dgreshel217@gmail.com
Facebook: facebook.com/david.greshel
Instagram: @electricinfamy
Twitter: @electricpoet217
Website: www.neonsunrisebooks.com

Additional Books by David Greshel and Neon Sunrise Publishing

Windows into the Past for the Camera Shy

Nomads, Pilgrims, Troubadours

Memoirs of a Broken People

NEON SUNRISE
PUBLISHING

Neon Sunrise Publishing is focused on helping independent creators realize their dreams of seeing their books in print. We're driven by a DIY spirit and a desire to provide options and resources to help developing talent succeed in sharing their voice with the world.

To keep up with all of our latest news and releases, be sure to join our mailing list and connect with us online!

Email: neonsunrisepub@gmail.com
Facebook: facebook.com/neonsunrisepub
Instagram: @neonsunrisepub
Twitter: @neonsunrisepub
Website: www.neonsunrisepublishing.com

www.ingramcontent.com/pod-product-compliance
Lightning Source LLC
LaVergne TN
LVHW041540070426
835507LV00011B/840